#1 INTERNATIONAL BEST SELLER

GUEST SPEAKER SUCCESS

10 PROVEN, INSPIRING SPEAKERS TO ELEVATE YOUR PLATFORM SUCCESS

#1 INTERNATIONAL BEST SELLER

GUEST SPEAKER SUCCESS

10 PROVEN, INSPIRING SPEAKERS TO ELEVATE YOUR PLATFORM SUCCESS

KEN WOOD AND KAREN CORBAN | JOHANN NOGUEIRA | CAROLYN APOSTOLOU
RUSSELL VOSS | SCOTT BAKER | ROB FLUX | PAULINE MARTIN-BROOKS
JANE SLACK-SMITH | MARTIN RENAUD | TIMOTHY CARROLL

By **Ken Wood & Karen Corban**, Johann Nogueira, Carolyn Apostolou, Russell Voss, Scott Baker, Rob Flux, Pauline Martin-Brooks, Jane Slack-Smith, Martin Renaud, Timothy Carroll

Edited by James North

Book Layout ©2023
Published by:
Evolve Global Publishing
www.EvolveGlobalPublishing.com

Guest Speaker Success: 10 Proven Speakers to Elevate Your Platform Success
1st Edition. 2023 - V3
Fonts: Minion Pro
Page size: 6" x 9"

ASIN: B0CPPFTN6M (Amazon Kindle)
ISBN: 978-0-6486231-4-4 (eBook)
ISBN: 978-0-6486231-5-1 (Amazon Paperback)
ISBN: 978-0-6486231-6-8 (Amazon Hardcover)
ISBN: 978-0-6486231-7-5 (Ingram Spark) PAPERBACK
ISBN: 978-0-6486231-8-2 (Ingram Spark) HARDCOVER
ISBN: 978-0-6486231-4-4 (Smashwords)

CONTACT THE AUTHOR
Business Name: Universal Stars Training Pty Ltd
Book Bonus: guestspeakersuccess.com
Contact: Ken Wood
Email: ken.wood@clientflow.marketing

TRADEMARKS

Table of Contents

Acknowledgements

Reflecting on the path that led us to this book, we are filled with gratitude towards the many remarkable individuals who have enriched our journey with their wisdom and support.

Our journey in the world of event promotions was profoundly influenced by marketing icon Jay Abraham, who introduced us to the powerful concept of host beneficiaries, also known as strategic alliances. This strategy alone has been a cornerstone in generating millions in revenue and amplifying our message to reach countless people.

We feel deeply grateful to the numerous strategic partners we've collaborated with over the years. These partnerships, founded for mutual benefit, have blossomed into enduring professional and personal relationships, significantly contributing to our collective business growth.

A special note of thanks goes to John North from Evolve Global Publishing, our publisher and collaborator. His innovative vision and guidance have been crucial in turning this book from a concept into reality.

Our heartfelt appreciation extends to the incredible teams we've had the privilege to work and co-create with over the years. Your collective efforts and dedication have been vital in transforming our visions into tangible successes.

We are equally thankful to the myriad of speakers we've promoted and consulted with over the years. The insights and concepts gleaned from these interactions have been pivotal in our personal and professional development.

To our coaches and mentors, your unwavering guidance has been our beacon through challenging times, keeping us focused and on course.

We extend our heartfelt thanks to all the clients we've had the honour of serving. Your trust and collaboration have been instrumental in our journey.

Our appreciation also goes out to the members of the Speakers Alchemy Network. Your generosity in sharing innovative ideas and strategies has elevated the success of other members, creating a ripple effect of achievement and inspiration across the community.

Lastly, our deepest gratitude is reserved for our parents. Your constant love, support, and belief in us have been the foundation of our journey, profoundly impacting our lives.

In the spirit of helping others grow, we recall the words of Napoleon Hill: "It is literally true that you can succeed best and quickest by helping others to succeed." This philosophy has been a guiding light in our mission, and we hope this book serves as a testament to that belief.

Karen Corban and Ken Wood

Introduction

Dear Event Host, Webinar Coordinator or Podcast Creator,

The book you're holding is the first of its kind, crafted specifically for you, to help make your work easier and more effective. This book, born from over three decades of Ken's and my rich experiences in the dynamic world of live events and webinars, is more than just a compilation of expert insights. It's a transformative resource designed to elevate your events into enthralling, impactful and lucrative experiences.

Our journey in this industry, fueled by a burning desire to foster growth through education and transformation, has been a thrilling adventure. We've been the catalyst behind disseminating powerful messages, representing speakers who have touched the lives of hundreds of thousands, guiding them towards success in various life aspects. We have witnessed over and over again what the right message can do for people delivered at the right time. It's simply life-changing!

Having promoted over 110 speakers across 7 countries, in events ranging from cozy gatherings of 10 to grand spectacles of 4,500 attendees and webinars with up to 1,500 participants, we've gained invaluable insights into this industry. This experience has honed our skills in selecting and collaborating with guest speakers and producing events that captivate and yield profitable outcomes.

Our mission is straightforward yet profound: to empower you, the event host, to expand your reach through selecting ideal guest speakers, strategic collaborations and impactful live events. We've seen first-hand the magic that unfolds when the right speaker synergises with the perfect event, and we're thrilled to share this contribution to your greater success.

This book distils our collective wisdom and that of nine other maestros in their respective fields. You'll explore diverse topics such as Partnerships, Collaborations, Leadership, Relationships, Beliefs and Mindset, Property, Health, the Power of Reviews, Audio Visual Strategies, and the Blueprint for Presenting Success and Maximising Sales at Events.

Consider each chapter a showcase of that speaker's knowledge, expertise, mission and style. While those attributes vary widely between speakers, they are all accomplished, committed, capable and profitable potential guest speakers for your in-person or online event. Each contributor offers a treasure trove of practical knowledge, having captivated audiences with messages that resonate and inspire.

You can evaluate the suitability of these speakers for your event based on their topic, content and message alone. Every speaker in this book will add value to your audience, respect the opportunity you've provided them, deliver on their promises with integrity and enhance the profitability of your event.

Whether you're orchestrating webinars, hosting podcasts or organising live events, this book is your partner in transforming events into experiences that leave indelible impressions on your audience. Welcome to a world where your events are unforgettable experiences for your audiences and pivotal milestones in your journey towards growth and success.

About the Speakers Alchemy Network (SAN)

In the ever-evolving world of speaking and events, filling events and sustaining a flow of leads and sales are daunting challenges. This is where SAN steps in, offering a revolutionary solution.

At SAN, a curated community of speakers and business owners, we recognise the power of collaboration in maximising sales and impact. Our network is dedicated to assisting speakers in forming strategic alliances, empowering them to grow their businesses and amplify their messages exponentially.

Joining SAN means entering a community of growth and opportunity. Here, you'll find a platform to exchange ideas, gain diverse perspectives, improve sales conversions and connect with like-minded speakers and coaches. We offer practical, actionable strategies, ensuring your success and growth in the speaking arena.

Your involvement in SAN is a guarantee of elevated success, equipping you to confidently navigate the speaking world's challenges. Join us, and let's collaborate to transform your events into unforgettable experiences that resonate with your audience and boost your profits.

Karen Corban

What Some of Our Members Say

"I learnt proven strategies to convert 60%+ of attendees to the next step of their development from live or online events. Strategies that I did not think were possible!

The diversity of this network is amazing, full of experienced business owners who are excelling in their chosen fields. I am looking forward to our continued monthly meetings and the growth & value to come."

TIMOTHY CARROLL, Carroll Consultancy Group

"I am one of the members of the Speaker's Alchemy Network, and it's been a really incredible experience. There are a few things that happen inside of the membership: Number one, we learn from each other. We get to present on our topic of expertise in front of the other members and vice versa.

By the way, the calibre of the members is just incredible. I've been around a lot of really amazing business owners, speakers, and experts, in my past and I'm quite simply blown away by every time I turn up on one of the calls.

I really love the learning, but also the second side is the masterminding. We help each other with our businesses. Because we all have our own business, we are all speakers and we're the public-facing person in our business, it's really helpful to be around people who have the same problems."

HEATHER PORTER, Website Love

"As a business owner, the main problem we have is the fact that many businesses can become a bit of a silo. As a result, you can start to lose energy, you can start to lose inspiration and you can find yourself getting into the humdrum of day-to-day work.

The biggest impact that the Speakers Alchemy Network has had on my business is being able to tap into effective and proven strategies that have come from many of the high-level networks within the group. To continue to build our flow of leads and customers coming into our business."

RIK SCHNABEL, Life Beyond Limits

"The biggest benefit I've seen since joining the Speakers Alchemy Network has been working with one of the biggest brands in the world. Before joining SAN, I don't even know how I would've been able to access that calibre of people, let alone be in the same room, let alone be introduced to them, let alone have a meeting with them. And that came from an amazing collaboration from two other members in the group."

SCOTT BAKER, Reviewology

The Authors

Ken Wood
Co-Founder of Speakers Alchemy Network, Founder of Clientflow.Marketing

Johann Nogueira
Entrepreneur, Tech Investor, Public Speaker

Carolyn Apostolou
Accredited Coach, Mentor, Speaker

Russell Voss
Qualified Social Worker, Master Practitioner in NLP, Energy Healer

Scott Baker
Creator of Reviewology and RevGenHub.com

Rob Flux
Founder of Property Developer Network and Development Sites Australia

Pauline Martin-Brooks
Strategic Partnerships Expert, Accountability Coach & Therapist

Jane Slack-Smith
Author, Founder of Investors Choice Mortgages, Your Property Success and Your Success Club

Martin Renaud
Founder of Freedom Potential Pty Ltd

Timothy Carroll
#1 Best-selling Author, Entrepreneur, Public Speaker

Chapter 1

The Blueprint to High-Profit Events: Strategic Presentation Design to Maximise Revenue

Ken Wood

Co-Founder of Speakers Alchemy Network, Founder of Clientflow.Marketing

About The Author: Ken Wood

Ken Wood is a "recovering engineer" turned marketer and entrepreneur. For three decades, he and his wife, Karen, have been passionate about helping people learn, grow and transform their lives through live events. Karen & Ken have produced thousands of events, including workshops, retreats, masterminds, seminars, webinars, summits and hybrid live/virtual events, for 10 to 4,500 participants.

After starting out in silicon chip design, then technical sales, Ken started his first business in the IT industry. Later, he joined Karen in her event promotions company, Universal Stars. Ken infused systems and automation into the business, paving the way for its rapid growth and expansion.

Together with their team, Karen and Ken grew Universal Stars into a leading Australian seminar promotions business. The company achieved milestones such as ranking on the Business Review Weekly "Fast 100" list in Australia for 3 consecutive years, as it delivered 1,208 live events in 7 countries, featuring 110 different speakers. In total, Universal Stars touched the lives of more than 500,000 people who attended its live seminar programs.

Ken's analytical bent led him to study event performance metrics such as attendance rates, conversion ratios, revenue per participant and profitability. From the data, he identified key success factors that create a memorable experience for the audience and move them to take action, thereby ensuring the event is profitable.

Today, Ken & Karen help to grow speakers' businesses through mentoring on marketing, business models or strategy, optimising their presentations and improving sales conversion rates.

They also co-founded and lead the Speakers Alchemy Network, the only professional group to provide education, peer support, networking and partnership opportunities for speakers who sell from the stage at in-person and online events. Members share a common, events-based business model, making the information shared within the group especially relevant and valuable to members.

Ken recently launched Clientflow, a sales and marketing automation software platform tailored for the unique needs of businesses conducting sales webinars and live events.

He can be contacted at *speakersalchemynetwork.com.*

★★★

Have you ever been amidst the electrifying atmosphere of a sold-out music concert? The kind where the energy is palpable, and you find yourself swept up in the moment, even splurging on merchandise just to hold onto that exhilarating memory a bit longer. Now, imagine harnessing that same energy and excitement for your own events.

If you've ever felt the thrill of a room (or a virtual space) buzzing with anticipation, you know the power of a live event. Whether you're a seasoned event host or just toying with the idea, there's a transformative energy in bringing people together, united by a shared purpose or interest. But how do you capture that concert-like fervour and turn it into a profitable venture for your business?

Imagine a world where every event you host not only elevates your brand but also consistently fills your programs with eager clients and boosts your revenue. Sounds great, right? Well, it's entirely achievable.

In the 22 years that Karen and I navigated the intricate maze of the seminar business, we've distilled a potent formula for event success. And now, I'm about to share this treasure trove with you.

With the strategy I'm about to unveil, you'll be equipped to:

- Magnetise a loyal audience, turning attendees into raving fans who amplify your reach and impact.
- Craft an irresistible offer, ensuring you have the ideal people in the room and present a compelling offer that invites them to continue their transformative journey with you.
- Transform your live events into a robust engine, powering your business with a steady influx of enthusiastic clients and predictable revenue.

Dive in, and let's unlock the secrets to optimising your events for unparalleled profitability.

Optimising Your Event For Profitability

Over the time when Karen and I ran our seminar business, we promoted 110 different speakers. Their experience ranged from beginners making their debut on our stage to some of the world's most renowned presenters and platform sellers. Each was exceptional in their own right, and I learned from every one of them. In this chapter, I'll share their strategies and approaches that consistently led to profitable events.

Front-End vs Back-End Events

I'll discuss two types of live events:

"Front-end" events aim to convert prospects into clients. Most attendees have likely only made a small purchase from you, like a book. Your front-end event offers them a low-cost, low-risk chance to get to know you and potentially make a purchase. The products you sell at your front-end event might include programs centred around a live event, such as workshops, retreats, or masterminds. I refer to these as "back-end" events: everyone attending is already a client, and you're fulfilling a promise made during their purchase.

You can also have something to sell at your back-end events. The way you deliver your offer will be different to your front-end events because trust has already been established and the attendees have learned more about you while immersed in your content. I like every event to be profitable in its own right, which means making enough sales at back-end events to more than cover all the costs.

Hosting Guest Speakers At Your Back-End Event

Given the title of this book, "Guest Speaker Success", let's delve into when and how to incorporate guest speakers into your events. I advise against having guest speakers at front-end events. Attendees are there primarily to connect with you. Introducing another speaker can dilute that connection and potentially impact sales. Reserve guest speakers for back-end events.

How To Maximise Sales Results For A Guest Speaker

Incorporating a guest speaker into your back-end event requires a careful balance. You want your guest speaker to establish rapport with the audience to ensure good sales, but without overshadowing your content or affecting your own sales.

After years of experimentation, here is the schedule that we found works best for a multi-day back-end event:

1. Announce your guest speaker during your introduction at the start of the first day, and edify them strongly. Mention them at other times during the event, e.g., remind attendees when they have another speaking slot coming up, and edify them at these times too.
2. Introduce your guest speaker by doing a 30–45-minute interview with them onstage, where you act as an advocate for your attendees and ask the questions they're most likely to want answered. The purpose of this segment is to help the guest speaker connect with your attendees and build rapport with them. You'll transfer your credibility and trust with the attendees to the guest speaker, elevating their perception of them far more rapidly than otherwise.
3. Make your guest speaker's first presentation content-only; no sales offer.
4. If there is time, make their next presentation content with a "soft offer" only, i.e. they can mention, almost in passing, that they have a sales offer and invite attendees to come and talk with them about it. But there is no pitch from the stage at this time.
5. Delay the direct sales offer until the guest speaker's last scheduled speaking slot. The goal is to allow attendees to connect with the guest speaker as much as possible before their sales offer.
6. Require the guest speaker to attend your entire event, to be there from their first (interview) segment until at least the end of the last day on which they speak, preferably until the end of the last day of the event. The guest speaker is encouraged to make themselves available to attendees during the breaks as well as before & after the event each day. The most successful guest speakers freely assist attendees with details of their content and thereby build relationships that contribute to later sales.
7. Avoid scheduling a slot for your guest speaker on the final day, if possible. Keep the final day free for your own sales offer, as it's the prime window for selling.

For a diagram showing ideal guest speaker scheduling for different event lengths, visit *https://guestspeakersuccess.com/guest-speaker-scheduling*

Typical Financial Arrangements For Guest Speakers

- The most common arrangement is a 50/50 net revenue share between the guest speaker & host.
- Guest speaker pays their own travel & accommodation costs.
- Guest speaker pays all costs to deliver the product or service sold.
- Host pays all costs of staging the event.
- Any revenue from future sales to clients acquired at the event goes to the guest speaker.
- It's advisable to price sales offers at, say, $2,000 or more to maximise revenue from the live event and provide a reasonable return to the host.

Ideal Front-End Event Structure

The length of your event plays a pivotal role in its success:

Short Preview Event: 2-3 Hours Up To 1/2 Day

A short preview event, lasting between two to three hours or up to half a day, offers convenience. The brief time commitment can make it easier to attract attendees. However, there are challenges to consider. Given the limited duration, it can be challenging to convince prospects that they will receive significant value from the event. As a result, many might perceive it primarily as a sales pitch. This perception makes it hard to justify charging for tickets, leading to an expectation that such events should be free.

The time constraint also limits the number of sales offers you can make, typically restricting you to just one. Selling from the stage becomes particularly challenging due to the limited time to connect with participants. Moreover, even minor hiccups or challenges during the event can have a disproportionate impact, potentially derailing the event and affecting sales outcomes. The potential revenue per attendee that can be produced is more limited than for longer events.

1-day Front End Event

A one-day event requires a more significant commitment from participants. However, the extended duration means attendees can more easily envision receiving substantial educational value, making them more inclined to purchase a ticket. In a typical event running from 9 am to 6 pm, there's ample opportunity to make two sales offers from the stage. Additionally, there's the possibility of having a back-of-room offer, such as premium coaching. The extended stage time simplifies the selling process, leading to more consistent results and a higher average revenue per attendee.

2-3 day Front End Event

Events spanning two to three days necessitate more advanced promotion to ensure participants can allocate time in their schedules. Successfully marketing such an event requires effective positioning, compelling marketing materials, and persuasive sales copy to achieve a satisfactory conversion rate. The primary advantage of this extended format is the opportunity it presents. The additional time allows for multiple sales offers, and with the right approach, it's feasible to achieve impressive conversion rates, especially with higher-ticket offers. The potential revenue per attendee for these longer events is notably higher.

Paid vs Free Front-End Events

Whether to charge for your front-end event or not is a topic that provokes heated debate among speakers! There's no one right answer. Free events are easier to get registrations for, but the people who register are less likely to show up on the day. Paid events are the opposite: your marketing must work harder to get registrations, but most of those who register will turn up. The best choice depends upon the length of your event.

- Shorter events of 1 hour to 1/2 day: definitely free. It's relatively easy to get registrations at an affordable cost, which helps to build your list, and about 30% to 35% will turn up for the event if you do a reasonable job with pre-event messaging and reminders.
- 1-day events: can go either way. A free event will see around a 25% to 30% show rate. I prefer paid events, which usually achieve about an 80% to 90% show rate.
- 2-day or longer events: definitely paid. A free event may see only a 15% show rate, while a paid event should get 80% to 90% show rate.

Strategic Presenting

Your presentation is pivotal to the financial success of your event. A sales-focused presentation differs significantly from a keynote or motivational talk. An effective sales presentation guides the audience through an emotional journey, culminating in them being receptive to your sales offer. It's a multi-step process that's more easily explained with the aid of a diagram and video commentary; you can find both here: https://guestspeakersuccess.com/presentation-design

Here are some key points to guide you in creating your presentation:

- Before you start planning your presentation, think about your client's end-to-end journey of transformation. Where would they end up if they learned everything you teach and had all the success you wish for them? For example, if you teach property investing, then you might take someone who's a complete newbie and doesn't know anything about investing all the way to becoming an accomplished investor with a large property portfolio, living off the passive income.
- Out of that years-long journey, what you teach at your event will comprise the first couple of steps. Then the sales offer you will make will take them another few steps further. Share that picture with your attendees early in your presentation. They may not have a clear vision of how far they can go, and showing it to them will excite them.
- At a high level, the presentation format involves teaching your attendees something useful to help them move forward on their transformation journey and helping them see for themselves that they've made progress. Then, make a sales offer to give your clients the opportunity to continue their journey with your help after the event is over.
- The purpose of a sales presentation is to prevent objections and evoke an ideal emotional state in attendees to make them receptive to the sales offer. Preventing objections is more important than handling them.
- The presentation flows through steps like validating dissatisfaction, fostering hope, encouraging rebellion from the status quo, forming new peer groups, getting pre-commitment, establishing the presenter's authority, building mastery/confidence, generating urgency, building trust, and recapitulating excitement before the sales pitch.
- New speakers often make the mistake of thinking about their presentation in two parts: teaching content followed by a sales offer. In fact, the sales presentation begins the moment you step on stage, even if you don't mention your product until many hours later. Everything you say & do from the start should include a deliberate intent to create sales when you reach the offer.
- Key elements for creating a receptive state for your sales offer include a clear vision of the desired outcome, well-defined goals aligned with desires, motivation, immunity to peer pressure, respect for the presenter's expertise, trust in the presenter, and a sense of urgency. The biggest obstacle is lack of self-confidence, so presentations benefit from including a primary goal of boosting attendees' self-confidence.
- The focus is to be on the attendees, first and foremost. The presenter can talk about themselves later in the presentation, for a limited time, after validating the attendee's situation and goals.
- Shorter presentations are harder to get right than longer multi-day events, and a short guest appearance at someone else's event is the most difficult

context of all to make sales. It's much easier to succeed at an event where the audience showed up to see you, where you have enough time to connect with the attendees and recover from any derailments.

Managing Participant Energy Levels

Your attendees are far more likely to buy if they're awake, alert and focused at the end of your presentation. Be constantly aware of their energy levels and include energy-boosting tactics at least every 30 minutes. Also, use one immediately if you sense participant energy levels falling too low at any time. Energy levels may slide during the breaks, which is OK; it's an opportunity to "rest" a little. But you must bring participants' energy levels back up during the event to enable them to progress with the emotional journey. Energy levels MUST be high for your sales offer to get maximum results.

Unavoidable Energy Downers: Compensate For Them

- Teaching dense or complex content.
- Showing the participants something negative or confronting about themselves or their situation.
- Presenting the participants with the unpleasant future on their current path.
- Logistical and administrative announcements.
- The post-lunch energy dip from digesting a meal.
- Teaching content that is only relevant to some participants.

Avoidable Energy Downers: Change The Behaviours

- Speaking in a monotone.
- Standing still for an extended period; no movement.
- Delivering boring content.
- Talking about yourself for more than a couple of minutes.
- A lengthy dialogue with a single participant from the stage.
- Delay in the presentation due to audio-visual or logistical problems.
- Participant discomfort due to lack of movement and a long wait for a toilet break.
- Participants are hungry or thirsty due to a late meal break.

Energy Boosting Tactics: Use One Every 20 Minutes, Minimum

- Tell a joke and make them laugh.
- High energy, positive music - especially on breaks.
- Physical movement, e.g. short stretch break, group massage.
- Participant interaction tactics from the stage; see "Engagement Tactics".

- Embedding content tailored specifically for the participants in your presentation, e.g. references to sports teams for that city (if you're visiting).
- Organise people (crew) to dance on stage during breaks.
- Play a "game show" type game, with prizes to win, as participants return from breaks.
- Group exercises, e.g. "Turn to your neighbour and tell them <something>".
- Walk among the participants and make eye contact or touch them (e.g. on the shoulder, shake hands).
- Tell a story that includes tension, excitement, drama or other strong emotion.
- Tell a story and leave off the ending (open loop), but make sure to deliver the missing end of the story later in the event.

Maintaining Participant Engagement

Here's a certainty about running a live event: if you leave your attendees to sit quietly in their seats throughout your presentation, and the first time you ask them to do something is to buy your offer... they most likely won't. You must keep your attendees engaged with your presentation, actively participating and following your instructions. Then, when you reach the end of your sales offer, and you invite them to buy, there's a far higher likelihood that they will.

Engagement Tactics: Use One Every 25 Minutes, Minimum

- Have them shout out when they agree with one of your statements.
- Ask them to raise their hands if they agree with you.
- Ask for head nodding and head shaking as yes/no in response to your statements.
- Have them call out a word to complete your sentence.
- Direct them to participate in group exercises: meet new people, share what you learned, compare your challenges, make a commitment, etc.
- Poll participants on brief questions, one after another, then repeat back their answers.
- Have them greet participants by name when they introduce themselves on the mic. (E.g. "Hi everyone, I'm Debbie". Participants: "Hi Debbie!").
- Teach them a unique phrase for the group to shout at specific times. (E.g. "Hoo-Ah!")

Each Time You Call For Engagement From Your Participants

- Ask for a response loudly and firmly.
- Be sure they know how to respond. If you've forgotten to teach them, then pause and show them before moving on.

- Mirror their response: raise your hand if you've asked them to raise their hands; call out the answer to the question along with them if that's what you asked for; etc.
- Acknowledge and reinforce their engagement with a "Thank you", "That's right", or similar.
- Remember that the first time you call for engagement, it's essential to establish a mutual understanding and connection with the participants. Don't move on until you've received a strong, energetic response. If response starts to trail off during your event, stop and repeat the call to ramp engagement levels up again.

Selling The Next Section

Each time you go to a break during your event (e.g., coffee breaks, meal breaks), there is a risk that some participants may choose to leave the event and not return. They are more likely to do this if the event is free, if they haven't found the event content relevant to their situation, if they're bored or simply not enjoying it.

These risks can be minimised by knowing your target client profile well and careful design of your ticket sales website & collateral as well as careful design of your presentation.

The other risk is if the participant isn't excited about your presentation content coming up after the break. They may not find the topic compelling, or you may not have told them what's coming up.

You can minimise this risk by including a mini "sales pitch" for the next session just before the start of each break, thus giving participants a reason and motivation to come back for that session. You can also preview the content of each session early in the day when you talk about the event schedule, but be sure to also remind participants right before each break so their memory is fresh as they walk out of the room.

Seeding Your Sales Offer

Subtly reference your programs throughout your presentation. This "seeding" process gently raises awareness of your offerings. For example:

"Now that you know how to get traffic to your website from Pinterest and SlideShare, the next step is to get those visitors to register for your webinar. When you get them on a webinar, you can engage with them more deeply, educate them about how you solve the problem they're dealing with and make a sales offer for your product. In my Blogging Profits workshop, I teach four different ways to collect Pinterest traffic opt-ins at a 15% or better conversion rate. Right now, I want to show you the fastest and easiest one of those tactics. It's usually not the highest converting of the four tactics, but it's fairly simple, and you can get it running in only an hour. Let's go...."

Seeding ought to be included from the beginning of your presentation design, as it ties into your choice of content to teach. Your objective is to seed each program you want to sell at this event at least once during your presentation. Seeding more often is better when you can.

Adding Trial Closes

Incorporate trial closes during your sales offer to gauge attendee reactions and highlight benefits. Don't overdo it: limit the number of trial closes you use and vary them; avoid using any trial close more than once per speaking block.

The place to add trial closes is right after you discuss a feature/benefit of your program, recount a client success story or give a client testimonial.

Here are some examples to start with:

- "Do you see how that would really help you?"
- "Does seeing that make you kinda excited?"
- "Wouldn't that make a huge impact if it happened to you?"
- "Do you think that's as awesome as I do?"
- "Isn't that awesome?"
- "Is that fantastic, or what?"
- "Isn't that great?"
- "That's pretty amazing, isn't it?"
- "What would it mean for you and your life if you <achieved result>?"
- "Can you see what that means?"
- "What a huge difference that would make, eh?"
- "Can you imagine what it would be like if you were getting that every single day?"
- "If the program only got you <small result>, would it be worth it? It certainly would be for me; I'd take that..."
- "If the program only got you one extra customer per week, would it be worth it? It certainly would be for me; I'd take that..."
- "The good news is that you'll soon be saying goodbye to <negative present situation>. Just think what that will be like. Incredible, huh?"

Common Mistakes & Tips For New Speakers

- Slow down. It's common for new speakers to want to cover too much ground in the available time, so they end up speaking too quickly. Maintain a pace that will allow your participants to fully absorb what you're saying. While you're an expert in this topic, it is new for them, and they need to process your words.
- Allow pauses for attendees to process emotions. It takes longer for a participant to feel an emotion than it does for them to understand intellectually. Imagine that you're a performer on stage, and after you deliver each line, the audience applauds. Wait for the applause to die down before speaking your next line.
- Cut your content in half, and then start planning your presentation timing in more detail. New speakers always overestimate how much content they can deliver in the time available. The actual figure is close to half what you first think.
- You're likely quite concerned about delivering maximum value to your participants, and rightly so. Remember that they will derive value from the whole experience of attending your event, not just from the amount of "stuff" you teach. Don't get hung up on teaching the maximum amount of content; instead, focus on delivering a holistic experience, of which the content is only one part.

Conclusion

Running live events, either in-person or online, provides immense leverage for growing your business revenue with minimal extra costs. The power of selling one-to-many offers a unique opportunity to not only expand your business but also touch the lives of countless individuals.

With the advent of AI, it's never been easier to research, plan and implement effective marketing strategies for live events and fill a (physical or virtual) room with your ideal prospects. Then, use the strategies covered in this chapter to deliver an event that is both impactful for attendees and profitable for you.

As a business owner or event planner, you can leverage the increasing popularity of virtual and hybrid events and the demand for personalised experiences. Now you can use event formats that expand your audience reach beyond geographical limits while also reducing your cost per attendee dramatically.

Live events are more than just a business strategy; they are also a vehicle to create lasting memories, foster transformative experiences, meet wonderful people, attract new business opportunities and leave a legacy that resonates long after the event concludes. I hope that you appreciate and cherish this unique form of human interaction as much as I do and that you enjoy great business success with it.

FREE BONUSES

The first step to running high-profit events is surrounding yourself with others on the same path and learning "What's working now" from them. The Speakers Alchemy Network is the only group dedicated to that, so I'm giving you a free one-month membership to see for yourself how it can propel you upwards towards your speaking goals.

Marketing is equally important to the success of your events and webinars, as the primary means to attract your ideal prospects to them. Clientflow marketing automation and CRM software is AI-enabled, making filling and running big, highly profitable events easy. Get a one-month free trial of Clientflow to see how it can revolutionise your speaking business.

Claim both of your free bonuses by visiting *https://guestspeakersuccess.com/profitable-event-blueprint*

Chapter 2

"You are ONE Deal Away" Redefining Success in the Age of AI

Johann Nogueira
Entrepreneur, Tech Investor, Public Speaker

About The Author: Johann Nogueira

Johann Nogueira is a visionary entrepreneur, tech investor, and public speaker with a profound love for sharing knowledge. In today's interconnected world, he believes that collective learning and shared experiences drive innovation and open new frontiers for prosperity.

Johann's expertise centres on developing and investing in technology that propels companies towards rapid growth and scalability. He knows that it's not just about what you do, but why you do it. For Johann, it's about maximizing impact in the limited time we have on this planet.

Since 2004, Johann has been at the forefront of the business world. He's nurtured enduring relationships with clients, including national brands, banks, and global companies. This extensive track record is a testament to the results he delivers.

Johann's journey began during his PhD at the University of Melbourne, where he discovered the power of systems and leverage. This pivotal moment led to the creation of a lead-generation-focused digital agency, followed by a nationally recognised building management mobile app.

Today, Johann is dedicated to teaching innovative business owners how to compress time through strategic use of systems and technology. His methods transcend economic conditions, transforming businesses into enduring assets that leave a legacy.

As a family man who values exploration and continuous learning, Johann embodies the principles he imparts. His story resonates with those seeking abundant, location-independent lives, while cherishing moments with loved ones.

Beyond his ventures, Johann is the founder of Business Authorities, a thriving community of business owners committed to mutual learning and philanthropy. Over three years, this movement has impacted over a million lives in need.

In 2019, Johann achieved a significant milestone by successfully exiting his building technology company. Now, with the emergence of AI, his latest venture, Comet Suite, promises to revolutionise lead generation. The platform is poised to become an indispensable resource for Business Development Managers seeking to identify and nurture their ideal clients.

Johann's narrative is a blueprint for business owners seeking to break free from constraints. Through his insights, entrepreneurs can build and scale their companies, secure in the knowledge that they are on a path to crafting their own legacies.

"You are ONE Deal Away" Redefining Success in the Age of AI

It doesn't matter if you are a start-up, a growing or an established company. Have you ever stopped and wondered just how close you are to that game-changing moment? You know, the one deal, that one connection, that could change the legacy that you leave?

Well, you're not alone. In fact, you're closer than you think. Let's talk about how a single connection can rewrite your destiny.

Elon Musk's Pivotal Call: The Tesla-Mercedes Partnership

In 2009, Tesla faced a critical juncture. The financial crisis loomed large, and Elon Musk sought a partner to secure the future of sustainable transportation. His target: Mercedes-Benz.

Elon, with unwavering determination, reached out to Dr. Dieter Zetsche, Chairman of Daimler AG. He proposed Tesla supply drivetrains and battery packs for Mercedes' B-Class Electric.

The pause that followed felt eternal. Zetsche, known for prudence, was considering the audacious offer. Finally, he replied, "Elon, this is intriguing. Let's explore this further."

This call marked a turning point. The Tesla-Mercedes partnership not only infused capital but also validated Tesla's technology globally. It set the stage for the ground-breaking Model S and reshaped the future of electric mobility.

Who is that one person that you would love to call that could change everything?

In these next few moments, I'll outline the purpose driven focus to bring these life changing deals into your world, and the exact systems you can use to make it happen.

But first… a back story as to why the ONE DEAL AWAY Mindset has shown me that it's the right path for anyone who's looking to grow.

When I had a start-up digital agency, one deal with another complimentary agency propelled my business forward to 6 figures. This one joint venture changed everything for my fledgling company and allowed me to acquire the resources and team I needed to grow. Years later, when I was in the growth phase in another company that I built, one deal grew my company to 7 figures in a couple of months, changing our course. The benchmark, my friends who had an established company that was turning over $700M/year, did one deal with an international company that gave them access to 2500 distributors, taking their company to a valuation of $1.2 Billion.

That "One Deal" can change the trajectory of your destiny and legacy.

We are about to embark on a journey; one of purpose and intention. I want you to not "by chance" meet the right people anymore, I want you to structure and plan to meet the best people in your world and make sure it happens. With every serendipitous connection, your business can grow just that little more (or exponentially) towards your end goal.

I want to take you on a journey that blends ancient networking wisdom with cutting-edge tech. Think of it as a turbo boost for your success journey. No more getting lost in a sea of faces at conferences, having coffee meetings with tire kickers or squandering time at events that lead to dead ends. We are intentionally flipping the script to focused success.

Napoleon Hill once dropped sage advice (Think and Grow Rich, 1937): "You are the average of the five people you spend the most time with." It's more than just a catchy phrase; it's a blueprint for building genuine connections.

We now live in the most connected age there has ever been. We have access to the greatest minds both past and present. A look into their daily lives, their resources, their people, their connections, their thoughts, their choices and their outcomes.

By leveraging technology and the power of AI, you're not just making connections; you're forging alliances with those who align with your goals. It's like having a compass that points unerringly to true north, guiding you towards collaborations that resonate with purpose. This is building your network with intent, with a clarity that ensures every interaction carries the potential for substantial returns.

Part 1: Building Authentic Connections

Know Your People!

In the realm of entrepreneurship and ventures, the value of real, human connections cannot be overstated. When like-minded individuals converge, a potent energy is unleashed, an energy born of shared passion, vision, and the collective pursuit of a common goal.

In such gatherings, there exists an almost palpable buzz; an electric charge that courses through the room. It's the resonance of dreams colliding, of minds synchronising, and of spirits aligning. This phenomenon is far from happenstance; it's the result of individuals feeding off each other's enthusiasm and zeal.

Imagine being part of a mastermind group, a collective of driven, innovative minds. Here, the exchange of ideas isn't merely transactional; it's a dance of intellects, a fertile ground for the germination of ground-breaking concepts. The excitement is infectious, propelling each member to stretch beyond their perceived limits.

In these environments, challenges cease to be burdens; they become opportunities for collective problem-solving. The setbacks that might daunt an individual are met with a united front; a surge of creativity and resourcefulness that knows no bounds. It's this dynamic that catapults your ventures forward at an exhilarating pace.

It's the human connections that bring an invaluable element to the table: accountability. When you're part of a network of like-minded individuals, there's an unspoken commitment to each other's success. Your triumphs become shared victories, and your challenges become shared burdens. This sense of mutual responsibility adds an extra layer of motivation, pushing each member to strive for excellence.

In essence, real human connections in ventures create a crucible of inspiration and determination. It's a space where ideas evolve into action, and action fuels momentum. It's a community where the sparks of innovation ignite into blazing trails of success. In this crucible, ventures don't just progress; they hurtle forward, propelled by the collective energy of individuals united by purpose and passion.

Now, let's find them :)

Leveraging AI As Your Digital Ally

In the age of digital connectivity, Artificial Intelligence (AI) emerges as a potent ally in the quest to find kindred spirits; the individuals who share your vision, values, and aspirations. By leveraging the power of AI, you gain a distinct advantage in not only identifying but also connecting with those who align perfectly with your goals.

AI operates on a foundation of data, sifting through vast troves of information to discern patterns and preferences. This computational prowess enables it to analyse not just individual characteristics, but also the nuanced intersections of interests and ambitions. It's akin to having a matchmaking service for professional collaborations.

Through AI, you can craft a profile of your ideal kindred spirit; a composite of traits, experiences, and goals that resonate with your own. This profile serves as a beacon, guiding the AI in its search across networks, platforms, and communities. It's a precision instrument, zeroing in on potential connections with a level of accuracy that far surpasses conventional methods.

Additionally, AI possesses the ability to scan not just individual profiles, but entire networks. It can identify clusters of individuals who exhibit the collective attributes of your ideal collaborator. This holistic view allows for a strategic approach, targeting groups or communities where your kindred spirits are likely to congregate.

These new tools can automate outreach, initiating conversations and facilitating introductions. By analysing communication patterns and preferences, they ensure that your interactions are not just initiated, but also crafted in a manner that resonates with your potential collaborator.

In essence, Artificial Intelligence becomes your personal networking assistant; a digital ally in the quest to find those who share your journey and vision. It operates with a precision and scale that would be impossible through manual efforts alone. With these tools, the process of identifying and connecting with ideal kindred spirits transcends chance encounters, evolving into a strategic endeavour guided by data-driven insights.

This is the most exciting part about the time we live in. In a matter of minutes, we can identify your ideal prospects/clients/ventures and have communication initiated with them in real time via various channels. We live in a connected world, and no one is out of reach anymore, no one!

At the end of this chapter, I will give you access to cutting edge tools that will allow you to leverage technology and connect with your ideal prospects/partners within seconds.

Solidifying Relationships

Building a real, enduring relationship with a potential life changing contact is an art that transcends mere transactions. It's about weaving a tapestry of trust, understanding, and mutual support - a bond that goes beyond surface-level interactions.

Communication serves as the lifeblood of this journey. It's not just about words; it's about meaningful exchanges that resonate with authenticity. It's about creating a space where ideas, aspirations, and challenges flow freely. In this exchange, both parties find not just answers, but a shared platform for growth.

Value is the currency of this relationship. It's about giving, not with the expectation of immediate returns, but with the knowledge that true partnerships are built on a foundation of mutual benefit. Whether it's offering support during challenging times, sharing insights gleaned from experience, or providing resources that propel their journey forward, every gesture solidifies your position as a trusted ally.

Active listening takes centre stage in this dance of connection. It's about more than hearing words; it's about understanding the deeper currents of their aspirations and needs. It's about tuning in to the nuances, the unspoken desires, and the underlying motivations. This skill transforms conversations from mere exchanges to powerful moments of resonance.

Celebrating milestones, both big and small, becomes a cornerstone of this relationship. It's about acknowledging achievements, no matter how incremental, and rejoicing in the progress made together. These celebrations are not just moments of triumph; they're affirmations of the shared journey, reminders that every step forward is a testament to the strength of the partnership.

And then there are the unexpected gestures - the small acts of kindness that leave an indelible mark of genuine regard. It's the surprise call to check in on their progress, the unsolicited recommendation that opens new doors, or the thoughtful gift that speaks volumes about your appreciation. These gestures go beyond the realm of business; they touch the heart, reinforcing the depth of the connection.

In this journey of building and solidifying a relationship with a prospect, you're not just creating a business ally; you're forging the path towards a best friend in the professional realm. It's a relationship built on a foundation of trust, fuelled by mutual support, and destined for long-lasting success.

Now you are ready to craft those deals with the right people and change your trajectory.

Part 2: The Power of AI Enhanced Networking

Picture a scenario where a hundred visionaries, each with a track record of achieving eight-figure success, converge in one room. What sets this gathering apart is that every attendee has been handpicked through the meticulous precision of AI. These aren't merely faces in the crowd; they represent potential collaborators, bound by a shared vision and ambition.

The connections forged in this environment transcend the realm of transactions; they are the seeds of ventures poised to redefine entire industries. This curated assembly of minds is a testament to the transformative power of AI driven networking. Would you like to be in this room?

One of the most revolutionary aspects of this technological leap is the emergence of personalised outreach. Fuelled by AI, this approach represents a paradigm shift in how we communicate and connect. No longer do we cast wide nets, hoping for a chance encounter. Instead, we engage in targeted outreach, ensuring our message resonates with pinpoint accuracy. Each interaction carries the potential for substantial returns, as it's delivered directly to individuals whose interests align seamlessly with our own. This newfound precision brings a level of intent and clarity to networking that was previously unimaginable.

The impact of AI enhanced networking extends far beyond convenience; it's a game-changer in the truest sense. The fusion of AI, big data analytics, and advanced algorithms not only streamlines the process of connecting with others but also elevates the quality and relevance of these interactions. It empowers us to navigate the expansive landscape of potential connections with a level of discernment and accuracy that was once reserved for the realm of science fiction.

In this digital age, the power of AI enhanced networking is not just a tool; it's a transformational force. It reshapes the way we approach professional relationships, opening doors to opportunities and collaborations that were once beyond our reach. It's a testament to the boundless potential of human ingenuity when coupled with the capabilities of advanced technology. With this newfound power at our fingertips, we're not just networking; we're forging the future of collaboration and innovation.

That "One life changing deal", is closer than you think. Are you ready?

Section 3: Maximising Returns: Turning Connections into Opportunities

Monetising Your Network

Turning your connections into business opportunities is a smart move. It's like finding hidden treasures in your network and using them to benefit everyone involved.

Napster and Facebook

One prominent example of turning connections into opportunities is the partnership between Mark Zuckerberg and Sean Parker, co-founder of Napster.

In the early 2000s, Parker, who had already made a name for himself with the creation of Napster, a pioneering peer-to-peer file-sharing service, crossed paths with Zuckerberg. At that time, Facebook was in its infancy, primarily serving as a social networking platform for college students. Recognising the potential for expansion and evolution, Parker mentored Zuckerberg, offering strategic advice, guidance, and valuable industry insights.

Under Parker's mentorship, Zuckerberg steered Facebook through a transformative phase. With Parker's help, the platform expanded beyond college campuses and onto the global stage, forever altering the way we connect and share in the digital age. Parker's industry connections and Zuckerberg's innovative vision laid the foundation for Facebook's explosive growth, eventually turning it into one of the world's leading social media giants.

This partnership is an exemplary illustration of how connections can evolve into substantial opportunities. Parker's mentoring not only enriched Zuckerberg's understanding of the industry but also facilitated access to invaluable resources and connections. It showcases the power of mentorship, collaboration, and leveraging connections to achieve ground-breaking success.

So, think about your connections. They are not just friendly chats; they can lead to successful businesses. They're like little seeds of opportunity waiting to grow into something big. Keep an eye out for how your network can become a treasure trove of possibilities. Who knows what amazing opportunities might be right around the corner?

Creating Win-Win Scenarios

Being a deal maker is an art of creating enduring value, where the emphasis is on establishing win-win scenarios that stand strong over time. It's not merely about closing a deal; it's about sculpting partnerships that leave both parties enriched and satisfied. This involves a thoughtful approach that considers the long-term implications of every agreement.

Consider the pivotal partnerships that have shaped your path. They aren't fleeting transactions, but rather, they represent collaborations where each party contributes distinctive strengths. By harmonising goals and values, you lay the groundwork for sustained prosperity. This alignment ensures that the interests of both parties are not only met in the short term but are also poised for growth and mutual benefit in the years to come. Real long-term friendships are forged when aligned.

True deal making transcends immediate gains; it's about building relationships based on trust and mutual respect. It's an investment in the future, where the success of one party bolsters the success of the other.

This cooperative approach lays the foundation for partnerships that endure market shifts and evolving business landscapes. It's a testament to the power of strategic thinking, where the aim is not just a single triumph, but a series of triumphs woven into the fabric of a long-standing, mutually enriching relationship. In essence, being a deal maker means architecting opportunities that continue to yield dividends long after the ink has dried on the initial agreement.

Long-term Relationship Management

Managing relationships for the long term and continuously adding value is a delicate art. It involves more than just initial enthusiasm; it requires ongoing effort to ensure the flame of connection continues to burn brightly.

A great example of long-term relationship management is Airbnb, a company that grew into a global powerhouse. Brian Chesky, Joe Gebbia, and Nathan Blecharczyk, the founders of Airbnb, started their journey in 2007. At the time, they were struggling to make ends meet, and they decided to rent out a spare room in their apartment to make some extra money. This sparked an idea: what if they could create a platform for people to rent out their homes to travellers?

As they embarked on this venture, they sought advice and mentorship from individuals who had experience in the tech and hospitality industries. One such mentor was Reid Hoffman, co-founder of LinkedIn and an established figure in the start-up world. Hoffman provided crucial guidance on scaling the business, user experience, and navigating the challenges of a rapidly growing start-up.

Over time, as Airbnb gained traction and began to disrupt the traditional hotel industry, the relationship between the founders and Reid Hoffman evolved. They moved from a mentor-mentee dynamic to a more collaborative partnership. Hoffman became an early investor and advisor to Airbnb, and his insights were instrumental in shaping the company's growth strategy.

As Airbnb continued to expand, it transformed from a small start-up to a global platform with millions of users. The founders, with Reid Hoffman's continued support, navigated through various challenges, including regulatory hurdles and scaling operations internationally.

The lesson, Airbnb's founders leveraged mentorship and strategic relationships to achieve substantial growth. The founders' ability to seek out advice from experienced mentors, like Reid Hoffman, and the mentor's willingness to invest time and resources, played a crucial role in Airbnb's evolution from a small start-up to a global disruptor in the travel industry.

To sustain relationships, active communication is paramount. Find people who see your vision and have built something significant that you can learn from. Regular check-ins, updates, and meaningful conversations go a long way in demonstrating your commitment to the connection. People love to help people and it's about showing genuine interest in the other person's journey and valuing their time and advice, both their successes and challenges.

This connection between people is NOT about taking as much from it as you can. It's more about giving into that relationship; think of it as depositing into a future bank account with an unlimited return.

This could involve sharing relevant insights, helping when needed, or even introducing them to beneficial contacts. The goal is to be a reliable source of support and enrichment in their professional and personal endeavours.

Celebrating wins, both big and small, is crucial. Acknowledging achievements, no matter how incremental, reinforces the shared journey and affirms the value each party brings to the relationship. This recognition fosters a sense of mutual appreciation and strengthens the bond.

Lastly, adaptability plays a pivotal role in maintaining long-term connections. Understanding that people evolve, and priorities shift allows for the relationship to grow and change organically. Being open to new opportunities for collaboration and exploration ensures that the connection remains dynamic and continues to add value to both parties involved.

In essence, managing relationships for the long term requires a blend of active communication, consistent value addition, celebration of achievements, and adaptability to change. It's about tending to the flame of connection so that it not only endures but also continues to illuminate the path to mutual growth and success.

Gratitude is key to success. When was the last time you reached out to the people who helped get you where you are and thanked them? You never know how many more people they want to send your way.

Give thanks, connect, add value and grow.

Section 4: Unlocking the Future of Business Enhanced by AI

The future of business is poised to be revolutionised by the integration of Artificial Intelligence. This transformative force is set to amplify the scope, efficiency, and impact of professional connections, ushering in an era of unprecedented possibilities.

AI's proficiency in processing vast amounts of data enables it to discern intricate patterns in individual preferences, professional trajectories, and industry trends. This proficiency empowers it to match professionals with precision, connecting them to opportunities and collaborators aligned with their goals. No longer confined to chance encounters, business with AI becomes a deliberate and data-driven endeavour, where the potential for meaningful connections is exponentially expanded.

However, it's important to acknowledge that while AI enhances networking capabilities, the human touch remains indispensable. Authenticity, empathy, and genuine connection are elements that cannot be replicated by algorithms. Instead, AI serves as a powerful tool, augmenting human efforts and expanding the possibilities within the business sphere.

The future of networking with AI is characterised by precision, personalisation, and foresight. The integration of AI into business platforms empowers professionals to make informed, strategic connections, positioning them for success in an ever-evolving professional landscape. As AI continues to evolve, so too will its impact on the way we conduct business, collaborate, and navigate our professional journeys.

Re-imagining SpaceX

Elon Musk had a grand vision of reducing the cost of space exploration and eventually enabling human colonisation of Mars. He founded SpaceX in 2002 with this ambitious goal in mind. However, turning this idea into reality was an immense undertaking that required the right team and significant time.

Musk assembled a team of some of the brightest engineers and aerospace experts in the industry. They worked tirelessly to design, build, and test the technology needed to revolutionise space travel. It took nearly a decade of hard work, experimentation, and overcoming numerous challenges before SpaceX achieved its first major milestone: the successful launch of the Falcon 1 rocket in 2008.

Over the years, SpaceX continued to push boundaries, successfully launching and landing reusable rockets, sending spacecraft to the International Space Station, and developing the Starship spacecraft for interplanetary travel.

Now, let's introduce the role of AI in this narrative. With the assistance of Artificial Intelligence, the process of assembling the right team and developing the necessary technology could be accelerated by a significant factor. AI-powered tools can analyse vast datasets to identify the most suitable experts and collaborators for specific projects. Additionally, AI-driven simulations and modeling can expedite the design and testing phases of spacecraft development, saving valuable time and resources.

In essence, by harnessing the power of AI, the journey from idea to a groundbreaking achievement like SpaceX's accomplishments can be accelerated by a factor of ten or more.

This not only opens new possibilities for innovation and exploration but also showcases the immense potential of AI in propelling humanity into a future where our boldest aspirations become reality at an unprecedented pace.

The Future is here…leverage it for your legacy.

Conclusion

You are "One Deal Away", in the rapidly evolving landscape of business, the integration of Artificial Intelligence (AI) emerges as a game-changer. It's not merely a technological advance, but a paradigm shift that expands the horizons of what's possible in building and nurturing meaningful connections. This technology ensures that interactions are not left to chance but are strategic and purposeful.

Yet, amidst this technological revolution, it's essential to remember that the human touch remains irreplaceable. Authenticity, empathy, and genuine connection are the bedrock of any fruitful relationship. AI serves as an invaluable tool, amplifying our efforts and broadening our reach, but it is the human element that infuses these connections with depth and meaning.

In essence, the future of business is a fusion of human ingenuity and technological prowess. By embracing the capabilities of AI, business owners unlock a new realm of possibilities, positioning themselves for success in an increasingly dynamic professional landscape. As AI continues to advance, so too will the potential for innovation and collaboration, reshaping the way we connect, collaborate, and thrive in the world of business and beyond.

To harness this power for your own success:

- Take a moment to reflect on your current network.
- Identify one valuable connection that you haven't been in touch with recently.
- Think of 'Who else is out there' that would be an amazing connection?
- Reach out to them with a genuine message.

*** **BONUS** ***

As promised, I want you to leverage the power of AI to speed up your success and close more of those deals that change your life and destiny. You can claim a free account of our AI powered lead generation software loaded with 100 credits, so you can find ideal connections for you to make that one life changing connection or facilitate that one deal.

Connect with me:

- Free AI Powered Leads account: Head over to http://cometsuite.com/one-deal-away to claim your account and get started on your journey towards strategic connections and transformative opportunities.

- Email me on johann@cometsuite.com

- Connect with me on Socials:
  instagram.com/johann.nogueira
  https://au.linkedin.com/in/johannnogueira
  https://www.facebook.com/johann.nogueira/

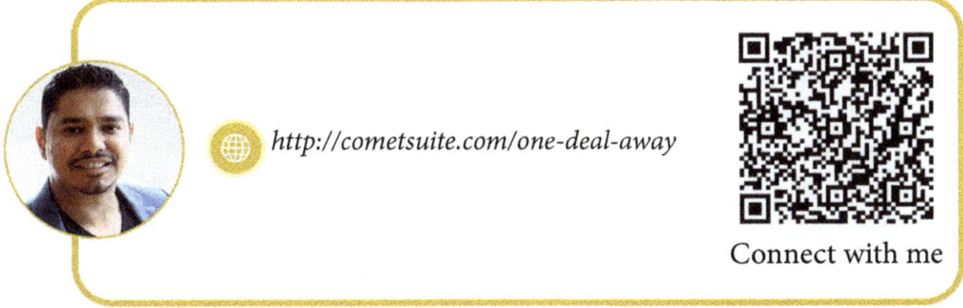

Chapter 3

Vital Health and Wellbeing Strategies for Preventing Burnout and Increasing Productivity in your Workplace

Carolyn Apostolou
Accredited Coach, Mentor, Speaker

About The Author: Carolyn Apostolou

Carolyn Apostolou is a true catalyst for change, renowned for her captivating keynote speeches that inspire transformation and empower individuals to prioritise their wellbeing. With years of experience in motivating leaders and teams, Carolyn has become a sought-after accredited coach, mentor, and speaker, addressing critical topics such as workplace wellbeing, stress management, and burnout prevention. Her dynamic speaking style and engaging presentations have earned her acclaim in the corporate world, making her a trusted expert in fostering thriving workplace cultures.

Drawing from her extensive experience as a teacher, school leader, and education advisor to prestigious institutions, including the International Baccalaureate and the Victorian Department of Education, Carolyn draws upon a wealth of expertise to deliver impactful keynotes that address burnout and empower leaders to create thriving, healthy work environments. Her compelling talks are informed by her qualifications in psychology, training, neuro-linguistic processing, timeline therapy, and hypnosis, making her a recognised authority in helping audiences overcome stress, avoid burnout, establish healthy boundaries, and reclaim their vitality and productivity.

In addition to her exceptional speaking abilities, Carolyn specialises in empowering staff and senior executives to create an organisational culture where success and wellbeing harmoniously coexist. Her impact extends far beyond the stage, fostering enhanced staff retention, productivity, teamwork, and collaboration, ultimately cultivating a flourishing company culture. Carolyn specialises in empowering staff and senior executives to champion corporate wellbeing and create an organisational culture where all employees feel seen, heard and valued. This results in enhanced staff retention and productivity, better teamwork and collaboration and a flourishing company culture.

Carolyn Apostolou stands as a beacon of inspiration, guiding individuals and businesses towards a brighter future. With her unwavering commitment to wellbeing, nurturing approach, high energy and ability to unlock the full potential of individuals and organisations, Carolyn inspires greatness and transforms workplaces into spaces where success and wellbeing can thrive in workplaces nationwide.

Are you feeling the heat of burnout with employees in your organisation? You're not alone. Burnout rates have been on the rise globally over the past few years, with the unrelenting pace of the modern world and the COVID-19 pandemic having made a significant impact. It can affect anyone, from stressed out career-driven people and celebrities to overworked employees and homemakers. Sadly, the consequences of burnout can be devastating.

In this chapter, we will explore burnout, its ramifications on employees within corporate settings, and present strategies and initiatives that can be implemented to prevent and address burnout in the workplace. Through real-life examples, expert insights, and practical tips, we will delve deeper into the various aspects of burnout and provide actionable solutions for both employers and employees. We will follow the story of Paul, who grapples with burnout in his organisation to provide a personal perspective on combating this important issue. Together, we can build a healthier, happier, and more productive workforce, ensuring the success and sustainability of businesses across Australia.

What is burnout and why is it affecting so many people today?

Life keeps giving me opportunities to share my passion for prioritising health and wellbeing. Sometimes this is with individuals in the playground at my children's school as we wait for the bell to ring; other times it's with busy corporate professionals who are burning the candle at both ends as they attempt to elevate their career. More often though, it's a desperate cry for help from a business owner struggling to retain their staff, dealing with decreasing job performance and escalating costs from employee absenteeism.

When Paul, a managing partner of a top-tier law firm in Melbourne, contacted me for help it was these issues that had him frustrated and desperately seeking answers. I met with him and his staff and it wasn't long before I could see the consistent pattern of burnout in his employees. Before delving into the specifics of Paul's situation, let's explore what burnout really is.

The term 'burnout' was first used in 1970 by Psychologist Herbert Freudenberger and Professor of Psychology Christina Maslach when they were investigating the prevalence of stress among mental health workers[1]. More recently, it has been associated with a much broader range of causes and has been applied across many

Footnote 1: *WB Schaufeli, MP Leiter & C Maslach, 'Burnout: 35 years of research and practice', Career Development Interational, vol 14, no 2, 2008, pp204-220.*

occupations. In 2019, the World Health Organisation (WHO) recognised burnout, categorising it as 'a syndrome conceptualised as resulting from chronic workplace stress that has not been successfully managed'.

Burnout is not just about feeling tired or stressed out; it's a state of chronic physical and emotional exhaustion, often accompanied by feelings of cynicism and detachment from one's work and a sense of ineffectiveness and lack of accomplishment. The WHO says the term burnout applies to workplace situations and should not be used to describe experiences in other areas of life. I beg to differ on this, though; anyone who has lived through the last few years of the COVID-19 pandemic can testify that burnout is far more far-reaching and diverse.

In Australia, the problem of burnout has been steadily growing. The demands of the modern workplace, increased workload, long hours, and pressure to meet targets have all contributed to this. According to research in 2022, nearly half (46%) of Australian workers are feeling burnt out[2], while in 2021, the American Psychological Association reported that 79% of employees had experienced work-related stress, including lack of interest, motivation and energy. The statistics by Deloitte and Workplace Intelligence are sobering[3]:

- A staggering 43% of workers reported feeling exhausted always or often.
- 42% were dealing with high levels of stress.
- 35% were struggling with overwhelming pressures.
- 23% reported feelings of depression.

But these challenges don't discriminate. They persist even in companies that offer ad hoc wellbeing initiatives. Why is this? Well, put it this way: whilst yoga classes, massages, and conferences have their place, they can't single-handedly reverse this tide.

So, what's the solution? Organisations need to be offering holistic solutions, not just temporary fixes.

In my professional opinion, organisations need better training and education for their teams, empowering them with stress management skills and resilience building. These tools are essential to preserving your employees' wellbeing and

Footnote 2: *2022 ELMO Employee Sentiment Index. The research was commissioned by ELMO Software and conducted by Lonergan Research between 11 March 2022 and 31 March 2022.*

Footnote 3: *https://www2.deloitte.com/us/en/pages/about-deloitte/articles/press-releases/new-deloitte-research-reveals-employee-well-being-worsening-at-some-companies-uncovering-a-pressing-need-for-greater-organizational-accountability-and-transparency.html*

helping them be their best. It's the businesses that are investing in strategic wellbeing strategies that are consistently outperforming the broader global market. So, it's a win-win – your team thrives and your organisation prospers.

Common Signs and Symptoms of Burnout

One of the first steps for business owners in addressing the burnout epidemic is recognising the signs and symptoms in their employees. These symptoms can be classified into three groups:

- Physical – feeling drained, frequent headaches or migraines, tight jaw, neck and shoulders, general aches and pains, low immunity, often sick, change in appetite, poor sleep patterns, often tired.
- Emotional – feeling undervalued, lack of self-worth, feeling trapped, unmotivated, cynical or negative, lacking purpose and direction, detached and disengaged, feeling defeated and lonely, emotional eating.
- Behavioural – social isolation, withdrawal from responsibilities, more absenteeism, being late for work, procrastination, avoiding difficult tasks, more errors, lack of mental clarity, reactive outbursts, frequent use of drug and alcohol to cope.

While there isn't a standard model for the stages of burnout, as people can have a totally different experience, burnout usually takes form in some of the following stages. In Paul's law firm, these signs were evident. Employees appeared physically drained, their enthusiasm for their work had waned, and interactions among team members were strained.

Stage 1: The individual works tirelessly to prove their value to the organisation.

Stage 2: The individual prioritises work, neglecting basic self-care practices.

Stage 3: The individual ignores their personal life, including family, social activities, hobbies, and health.

Stage 4: The individual may notice signs but ignores them or just keeps pushing through and is disconnected emotionally.

Stage 5: The individual feels empty, lacks direction and purpose. They may turn to substances or bad habits to cope.
Stage 6: This progresses to depression or anxiety due to poor mental health.

Stage 7: The individual may reach a crisis point, experience panic attacks, leading to mental, physical, and emotional burnout.

All of this can be managed or prevented the quicker the workplace and/or individual becomes aware of it.

Preventing Burnout - Strategies for Organisations

Having worked with many different organisations, the responsibility for preventing employee burnout rests heavily on the shoulders of the employers. If employees reach the end of their fuel tanks with an organisation, it's likely they will look for better opportunities elsewhere. This is obviously not ideal. So, what can organisations do to better support their staff, increase retention rates and attempt to prevent employee burnout?

It can't be stressed enough that the best cure for burnout is prevention. It's on managers and organisations to protect their employees from becoming resource-depleted in the first place, and it's also on the employer to provide the resources necessary to support employees' mental health.

The Ripple Effect

When employees experience burnout, it doesn't just affect their personal wellbeing; it has a profound impact on the workplace as well. Productivity takes a hit, creativity wanes, and the overall work atmosphere becomes toxic. This, in turn, affects client relationships, as burnt-out employees struggle to provide the level of service and dedication that clients expect. As I sat down with Paul and his team, it became apparent that this ripple effect was hitting his law firm hard.

Paul's story is not unique. Many business owners across Australia are facing similar challenges. The fast-paced, competitive nature of today's business world often pushes employees to their limits, leaving them with little time or energy for self-care. As a result, burnout has become a pervasive issue, affecting employees in various industries, from healthcare and education to finance, technology and professional services. Addressing burnout requires a comprehensive approach that focuses not only on individual wellbeing but also on reshaping the workplace culture.

Shifting the Workplace Culture

Creating a workplace that promotes health and wellbeing is essential in preventing and addressing burnout. It starts with leadership. Business owners and managers play a crucial role in setting the tone for the workplace. Fostering a culture that values work-life balance encourages open communication and provides adequate support, employers can significantly reduce the risk of burnout among their employees.

In Paul's law firm, we initiated a series of strategies to realise this vision. We encouraged work-life balance by offering flexible schedules, remote work options, ensuring staff take their leave, allowing employees to manage their personal and professional lives effectively. This approach, combined with opportunities for professional development and growth, ensured that employees remained engaged and motivated.

Furthermore, we fostered a culture of open communication and feedback, where employees felt comfortable addressing concerns and issues before they could escalate. We also ensured employees had all the necessary resources and support to perform their jobs effectively, removing potential obstacles that could lead to burnout. Paul consistently showed appreciation and recognition for employees' hard work and contributions, reinforcing their value and motivation within the organisation.

To complement these strategies, I ran a series of workshops and training sessions focused on stress management, time optimisation, and resilience building. These sessions equipped employees with practical tools to cope with workplace pressures effectively. Additionally, we encouraged regular check-ins between managers and team members to assess workload, identify potential stressors, and provide necessary support.

Through this comprehensive approach, Paul's law firm aimed to create a workplace that prioritised employee well-being and reduced the risk of burnout, ultimately fostering a healthier and more productive work environment for all.

The Importance of Self-Care

Promoting self-care is another vital aspect of combating burnout. Encouraging employees to prioritise their physical and mental health both improves their overall wellbeing but also enhances their resilience in the face of challenges. In Paul's firm, we introduced yoga sessions, meditation classes, and access to counselling services. These initiatives aimed to empower employees to take charge of their health and equip them with coping mechanisms to deal with stress effectively. I personally conducted a series of sessions that covered the following simple practices of self-care:

1. Hydration – the importance of water

The importance of water intake for our body can't be ignored. Yet, it's one of the most overlooked aspects of self-care. The human body is made up of between 50-80% water. All the body's chemical processes take place in water and that's why it's essential for good health. As a coach, I often find so many people don't get enough water. Dehydration can lead to fatigue and reduced cognitive function, making it more challenging to manage stress.

If you think you need to be drinking more, here are some things I like to do to increase my fluid intake and reap the benefits of water:

- Aim to drink one litre of water by 11am and a second litre by 2pm.
- Have a glass of water with every snack and meal.
- Eat more fruit and vegetables. Their high water content will add to your hydration. About 20% of our fluid intake comes from foods.
- Keep a bottle of water with you in your car, at your desk, or in your bag, really making a conscious effort to drink water throughout the day.

Drinking more water each day is a small but significant step in preventing burnout.

2. Nutrition – fuelling the body and brain

Nourishing your body with healthy food is vital for maintaining your energy levels, enhancing focus, promoting overall wellbeing and combating burnout. Nutrient-rich foods provide the body with the energy and vitamins it needs to function optimally.

Here are some healthy snack ideas that will fuel the body and brain with nutrition:

- Nuts and seeds – Get a zip lock bag and fill it with your favourite nuts and seeds or buy a natural trail mix.
- Boiled eggs – Containing 98% protein, they are great for brain function.
- Berries – Full of antioxidants and vitamins, they are the perfect touch to add that little sweetness to your day.
- Brown rice cakes and avocado – Brown rice cakes are an excellent, shelf-stable snack for the office. Avocados are high in healthy fats and fibre.
- Apples and peanut butter – This combination makes for a delicious, satisfying snack. Peanut butter contributes protein and healthy fats, while apples are high in fibre and water, making them particularly filling.

If consistently fuelling your body and mind is an area you know you struggle with, here are some practical nutrition tips:

1. **Plan Ahead:** Spend a few minutes each week to plan your meals and snacks. Prepare a grocery list and ensure you have nutritious options readily available. Consider batch-cooking meals that can be enjoyed throughout the week, saving you time and effort.

2. **Pack Your Meals**: Taking control of your nutrition starts with bringing your meals to work. Pack a balanced lunch and snacks, including lean protein, whole grains, and an assortment of colourful fruits and vegetables. This will help you avoid relying on unhealthy fast food options or vending machine snacks.
3. **Don't Skip Breakfast:** Breakfast is the fuel that kick-starts your day. Aim for a nutritious breakfast that includes a mix of complex carbohydrates, protein, and healthy fats. Oats, smoothies, or Greek yoghurt with nuts and fruits are convenient and nutritious options.
4. **Smart Snacking**: Choose smart snacks to curb hunger and keep your energy levels stable throughout the day. Opt for options like fresh fruit, raw nuts, yoghurt, or pre-cut vegetables with hummus. Keep healthy snacks in your desk drawer or bag, so you're less tempted by less nutritious alternatives.

Remember, small changes in your daily routine can lead to significant improvements in your overall nutrition. By prioritising healthy eating habits, you'll fuel your body for success, enhance your professional performance and reduce your risk of burnout.

3. Exercise – moving towards wellbeing

Exercise can reduce stress and anxiety, improve mood, increase productivity and boost energy levels. But, let's face it...with our demanding work schedules, it's easy to find ourselves glued to our chairs for long stretches of time. Here are some strategies to help you break free from the sedentary trap and create a healthier work environment reducing your risk of burnout:

1. **Stand Up and Stretch**: Take regular breaks to stand up, stretch your muscles, and improve blood circulation. Set a reminder or use tools like Pomodoro technique to encourage short activity breaks every hour.
2. **Walk and Talk**: Whenever possible, opt for walking meetings or phone calls. Get up from your desk and take a stroll while discussing ideas. Not only will it get you moving, but it can also boost creativity and productivity.
3. **Deskercises**: Incorporate desk exercises into your routine to keep your body active. Simple stretches, chair squats, or leg raises can be done discreetly and help prevent muscle stiffness.
4. **Take the Scenic Route**: Instead of using the closest bathroom, choose a more distant one. This way, you'll add extra steps to your day and break the monotony of sitting.
5. **Stand-Up Desk**: If feasible, invest in a standing desk or a sit-stand workstation. Alternating between sitting and standing throughout the day can significantly reduce sedentary behaviour.

Remember, small changes around your daily movement can make a big difference when it comes to promoting physical activity and movement in the workplace.

4. Sleep habits – the importance of rest

Do you ever go to bed saying to yourself, "Tomorrow is the day that I'll wake up when the alarm goes off?" And then the clock strikes six, the alarm buzzes, and you fumble around looking for the snooze button. A person's circadian rhythm regulates when their body sleeps and wakes. Various factors such as travel, shift work, and frequently staying up late can disrupt the circadian rhythm. Quality sleep is essential for overall well-being. Burnout often disrupts sleep patterns, leading to a vicious cycle of exhaustion.

Here are some ways you can reset your sleep schedule:

1. **Set a consistent routine**: waking and sleeping at the same time every day. If you find it difficult to achieve this, try gradually changing the time you go to sleep by 15–30 minutes until you reach your goal.
2. **Use light and dark:** Light levels have a significant impact on the circadian rhythm. Try getting exposure to natural daylight upon waking and using softer lighting in the evening.
3. **Exercise in the morning:** A busy schedule means more and more people are exercising in the evening. This can disrupt sleep because exercise wakes the body up. If possible, try shifting the exercise to the morning.
4. **Eat early:** Eating large meals late at night can make it difficult to sleep. Try eating evening meals several hours before bedtime and avoid caffeine and alcohol in the evening as both reduce sleep quality.
5. **Spend time unwinding**: Working into the evening or feeling stressed may make it more difficult to get to sleep at a suitable time. Make a to-do list for the following day and avoid looking at screens prior to bedtime.

Quality sleep is absolutely vital for burnout prevention.

5. Mindfulness – cultivating inner peace

We all recognise the need to slow down and be more present in our daily lives, but it's easy to forget. Incorporating mindfulness techniques like deep breathing, meditation, or staying present during short breaks can reduce stress, improve focus, and build resilience. These practices can help you regain clarity, restore energy, and prevent you from feeling overwhelmed and burnt out.

As a coach, I often get asked..."How can I bring more mindfulness into my everyday life?"

Here are some strategies I find most effective:

1. **Meditation minutes:** This is a wonderful practice for times when you start to feel a little stressed or aggravated. It's a wonderful way to switch off and calm your thoughts. Use your phone to set a timer and focus your entire attention on your breathing, and nothing else. There really are no rules when it comes to a perfect time to meditate, but I find that for me, early morning is best before the household is awake and before the day begins. It also sets your day up in a positive headspace.
2. **Eat with awareness**: Mindful eating has been shown to aid weight loss and healthy digestion. When you sit for your meal, turn off all distractions and focus on your immediate experience.
3. **Mindful walking:** Be present in your here and now experience. Aim to be there for every step embracing the subtle sensations beneath your feet and the rhythm of your breath, connecting deeply with the present moment.
4. **Journalling**: When we write things down, we are forced to articulate what we're feeling and this can give you a new perspective on anything that has been troubling you and help clear your mind. Taking this time (even if it is only 5-10 minutes) can really help you sort out your thoughts and offload some of those things you seem to carry.

A little more on journalling…

To help you with your journalling, I've included some prompts to help you know what kind of things to write about.

- What are 3 things you're grateful for today?
- What is one thing you would like to do well today?
- What is working well in your life right now?
- What helps you feel the most relaxed?
- What breakthroughs have I had recently?
- What will I do to take care of myself today?

Hopefully, these prompts spark something inside of you to put that pen to the paper and let the words flow.

6. A morning routine – to start your day well

I love starting my day peacefully before the chaos begins. I like to use this time to do something good for myself before anyone or anything else. This sets a positive tone for the day, preparing me for the day's challenges. I enjoy helping clients create a simple morning routine for self-care without overwhelming them. It's a great way to reset, especially if life feels overwhelming. It's quick, easy, and most importantly impactful.

1. Take 5-10 slow, deep belly breaths
2. Listen to 5 minutes of meditation
3. Eat a balanced and nourishing breakfast and make sure you chew your food well
4. Hydrate with a big glass of water
5. Say out loud 2-3 things you are feeling grateful for
6. Make a list of priorities for the day

General advice for individuals

From my work with clients, there are a few final tips that I would like to share with you to help you prevent burnout.

1. **Set Clear Boundaries**: Establishing boundaries between work and personal life is crucial. Designate specific times for work and leisure activities, and stick to them. Avoid checking emails or working during off-hours, allowing yourself time to recharge.
2. **Prioritise Self-Care**: Don't neglect your own needs. Engage in activities that bring you joy and relaxation, such as exercise, hobbies, or spending quality time with loved ones. Remember, self-care is not selfish; it's essential for your overall wellbeing.
3. **Seek Support:** Seeking support from others can also be incredibly helpful when dealing with workplace burnout. Talk to trusted colleagues, friends, or family members about your challenges. Consider working with a corporate wellness coach or seeking professional counselling for additional support and guidance. Remember, you don't have to face burnout alone.
4. **Manage Workload:** Asses your workplace and identify tasks for delegation or simplification. Prioritise and communicate limits to superiors. Maintain a balance between challenging projects and manageable workloads. My to-do list is my trusty sidekick. I prioritise tasks, ensuring I tackle the most critical ones first. Allocating specific time blocks for tasks is like having a superpower, it keeps distractions at bay and ensures I'm focused on one thing at a time.
5. **Cultivate a Supportive Work Environment**: Advocate for a positive work culture that promotes employee wellbeing. Encourage open communication, teamwork, and work-life balance within your organisation. By fostering a supportive environment, you contribute to a healthier workplace for everyone.
6. **Tech Breaks**: Implement tech detox hours. No screens before bed is a great way to improve sleep quality and overall wellbeing.

Remember, preventing burnout requires a proactive and holistic approach. By taking care of yourself, setting boundaries, and seeking support when needed, you can overcome workplace burnout and show up as your best self in both your personal and professional life.

Conclusion:

Addressing the growing problem of burnout in Australian businesses requires a collective effort. Employers, employees, and policymakers must work together to create a supportive environment where individuals can thrive both personally and professionally. As I left Paul's law firm after several months of implementing these changes, I could see a transformation taking place. The once exhausted and demotivated employees were now more energised, engaged, and resilient.

While the journey to overcoming burnout is undoubtedly challenging, the positive impact it has on individuals and organisations is immeasurable. By prioritising the wellbeing of employees, businesses not only retain their valuable talent but also create a workplace where people are motivated, fulfilled, inspired to achieve their best and increase profitability.

Burnout is a significant concern but it is not insurmountable. Paul's story with his employees illustrates that with the right support and self-care strategies, individuals can recover from burnout and build resilience.

Bonus items/gifts:

Go to https://carolynapostolou.com.au/ and book a free corporate or individual health check worth $500.

Get a FREE copy of Your Morning Mindset Accelerator:
https://pgth4buxcxj.typeform.com/to/hs0euswL?typeform-source=linktr.ee

Grab this FREE recipe book of nourishing meal ideas:
https://view.flodesk.com/pages/61e897654cfe7529d668b5c0

Keynote Speaking:

Book Carolyn Apostolou for your next event, webinar or podcast.

Email: info@carolynapostolou.com.au or call 0417 572 775

Some topics to consider Carolyn for include:

- Leadership and Burnout Prevention
- Effective Stress Management
- Mental Health at Work
- Resilience Building
- Work-Life Balance
- Mindfulness and Wellbeing
- Time Management and Productivity
- Employee Wellness
- Remote Work Management
- Team Building Focus

Chapter 4

The Wake-Up Call: Facing the Hard Truths of Your Relationship

Russell Voss
Qualified Social Worker, Master Practitioner in NLP, Energy Healer

About The Author: Russell Voss

Meet Russell Voss, affectionately known as Russ, a transformative force in personal development, mental health, and relationship therapy. With over three decades dedicated to psychology, neuroscience, and metaphysics, Russ stands out as an expert that transcends traditional therapy methods. His approach is a holistic lens on human behaviour, setting him apart as a true trailblazer in his field.

His formative years were spent in a pivotal six-year term in the Royal Australian Navy, an experience that instilled a deep sense of discipline, compassion, and a zest for adventure. At 40, a significant life 'correction' led him to earn a Bachelor of Social Work. This educational journey catapulted him into a variety of roles, from crisis centres to healthcare settings, and even community services in Australia's remote regions.

Russ has educated audiences in Victoria and Tasmania, focusing on the crucial issue of suicide intervention and prevention. This work is close to his heart, but his broader mission is monumental: to reach millions of people with the aim to transform the culture of 'disposable' relationships and significantly lower Australia's concerning divorce rate. His mantra is as straightforward as it is impactful: "I don't just guide you; I help you understand why it's beneficial to follow the path."

Russ is not just a Qualified Social Worker. He is also a Master Practitioner in Neuro-Linguistic Programming (NLP) and an Energy Healer, a unique combination that adds unparalleled depth to his methodology.

His mission is singular but profound: to assist men and their partners in transforming their relationships, rediscovering happiness, becoming exceptional role models for their children and contributing to a more harmonious and balanced world.

Russ isn't just running a business; he is spearheading a movement. His forthcoming book, "The 7D's: Your Guide to a Dream Relationship," stands as a testament to his lifelong commitment to enriching relationships and enhancing lives.

Looking for a speaker who can transform, inspire, and educate your audience on 'Creating Dynamic Relationships'? Look no further than Russell Voss. With Russ, your audience won't just listen—they'll experience a transformation.

The Thunderbolt Moment

Picture this: you're a successful guy aged from 35 up, and life and your relationship seems fine. Then BAM! a lightning bolt strikes—divorce papers land on your kitchen table. It's jarring, like a gut punch you never saw coming. You wonder, "Where did it all go wrong?" You aren't alone. Many men, like you, ignore the telltale signs until the hammer drops. But take heart—this is your wake-up call, a chance for a course correction before you hit rock bottom. Did you see the signs? Did you notice the silent alarms?

The Silent Alarms

You're a father of two, tiptoeing around the house, fearing the next explosive argument. It's not just draining; it's a soul-crushing experience. These aren't random speed bumps; they're glaring red lights indicating your relationship is in critical condition. Your kids feel it too, and they're absorbing this toxic environment as their 'normal,' which could have long-lasting effects. Did you fear the power or tip the balance of power?

The Balance of Power

Are you the peacemaker, the one who always gives in to avoid conflict? It's not harmony; it's you waving a white flag. When your opinions are dismissed or flat-out ignored, it's a power imbalance that's shaking the foundation of your relationship. And what does that tell your children about respect and equality?

The One-Man Show

If you're juggling all the household chores, the finances, and the emotional labour, you're not a partner; you're an unpaid intern in your own home. When you're described as "the chef" instead of an equal, that's not just an insult; it's an alarming sign that your relationship is a one-man show. Is it time to realign your values or live them?

Clash of Values

Values are the bedrock of any partnership. When you're pushing for honesty and your partner is dishing out deceit, it's like you're living on different planets. What lesson does this teach your children? That it's okay to compromise their values for the sake of peace?

The Hidden Scourge: Abuse

Abuse, whether emotional or physical, is intolerable. Living in a state of constant alert, waiting for the next emotional grenade, is a life no one should endure. These scars are not just skin-deep; they're traumatic memories imprinted on your children's minds.

The Financial Storm

Divorce isn't just the end of a relationship, it's a financial apocalypse. Between legal fees, asset division, and child support, you're staring at a financial black hole. This isn't just about dollars; it's about the emotional capital you've invested and stand to lose. Are you just ousted from the bedroom or our of balance?

The Intimacy Drought

When your bedroom becomes a no-go zone, it's a crisis. Physical intimacy is more than just a biological need, it's the emotional glue that holds a relationship together. Without it, you're not a couple, you're just two adults sharing a living space. Is it time to listen to reason?

The Reality of "I Do"

Marriage isn't a fairy-tale ending; it's a never-ending story of challenges. If you think the wedding was the finish line, you're in for a rude awakening. Marriage is a daily choice to stay committed, to work through the bumps and continue on the journey together, through thick and thin.

The Brutal Truth and The Way Forward

Ignoring these signs sets you on a path toward becoming a grim statistic in the divorce rate. But there's an alternative—a path of action and change. Stick with me, and let's turn these red flags into stepping stones for a stable, fulfilling, and mutually respectful relationship.

Why Listen to Me?

I'm not just another therapist. I've navigated these choppy waters and led men back to safer shores. I offer transformative solutions, not just band-aid fixes. I understand because I've lived it, and I can guide you through this labyrinth to a better place.

Meet the Man Who's Walked Your Path: How My Journey Can Transform Your Relationship

Hi…I'm Russell Voss, and if you think you're alone in the struggles you face in your relationships or life, think again. I've had my fair share of ups and downs. In fact, my personal experience with relationships has been, let's say, 'interesting,' but those experiences have been invaluable. They led me to the fulfilling relationship I have today. I've been diving deep into the human mind's mysteries since 1987. That's not just a few years; that's decades of looking under the hood, figuring out what makes us tick.

But why should you listen to me? Let's get into it.

Back in 2000, I discovered the power of energy healing. This was no small thing; it was a game-changer. It shifted how I saw life's challenges and how I reacted to them. The impact was so profound, it felt like I found my life's purpose. I knew then that I wanted to use what I'd learned to help others.

Fast-forward to 2004, and I found myself as a volunteer at a crisis call centre. Imagine being the only light in someone's pitch-black tunnel. That was me, helping people through their worst moments. This was the stepping stone to more significant roles in suicide prevention and intervention. I didn't just stop there; I went on to educate communities in Tasmania and Victoria (Australia) about these life-saving topics.

As the years rolled on, I got my Social Work degree. This added a whole new layer to my understanding of people and relationships. I've been a guiding hand for stroke survivors, visited businesses as an employee counsellor, and even worked in public health across all the different departments. Whether it's reconnecting families in Remote North Queensland or counselling individuals with challenging behaviours, my work has touched all corners of human experience.

You're a successful 35+-year-old guy, with kids. You've got the house, the car, but you're missing peace at home. I get it. I've seen men like you rediscover what made their relationship magical in the first place. I've seen them become heroes in their children's eyes. That's what I want for you.

Why am I sharing all this? Because I'm not just rattling off textbook stuff here. I'm drawing from a deep well of experiences that span different fields and decades. In my current role as a Relationship Therapist, I bring together my skills as a qualified Social Worker, Master Practitioner of Neuro Linguistic Programming (NLP), and Energy Healer. My endgame? To help you and your partner find that lost magic and be fantastic role models for your kids, resulting in me, doing my part, in contributing to a happier world.

I'm always learning, always growing. That means you get the benefit of the most up-to-date techniques and insights. My dedication to growth ensures you get the best care possible, both effective and compassionate.

So, do I have the authority to guide you through your relationship maze? Absolutely. But more importantly, I have the dedication and the passion to help you turn your relationship struggles into stepping stones for a happier, stronger relationship.

"I Get It: The Heartbreaking Reality and the Way Out"

Ok, have you ever felt like you're walking on a tightrope in your relationship? One wrong step, and down you plummet into an abyss of arguments, misunderstandings, and, God forbid, betrayal. Trust me, I've been there—stuck in that downward spiral. I've also been the lifeline for many men who've walked through my office doors, desperate for a way out.

Imagine this: you're standing at the altar, like many guys have said to me, and your bride-to-be is walking down the aisle towards you. This is supposed to be the pinnacle of happiness in your life, right? But then, reality gives you a sharp jab in the gut: "What am I doing here? What have I just committed to?" Escape is not an option. Your family and friends are all present, their eyes laser-focused on you, anticipating your "I do." It's a dread-filled moment that can set you on a journey you never intended. But you do what blokes are supposed to do, so they say and you just bury it, smile, and continue on.

We've all mastered the art of self-deception. "She'll change," "The fights will stop after the kids arrive," "Things will improve over time." These comforting lies slowly chip away at our peace of mind. I've had sessions with clients—and let's be honest, I've been that client—who made the decision, for one reason or another, to not father any more children, and, have this agreed to, only to have their partner completely change the rules as soon as the wedding bells stop ringing. The weight of that betrayal is immense, like carrying a boulder on your back.

Let's cut to the chase. The burden you're carrying is massive, especially if you're a father. It's not just you and your spouse; it involves your children, your hard-earned assets, and your entire future. And don't even get me started on the broken Child Support System—an intricate, frustrating maze that you wouldn't wish on your worst enemy.

Speaking of children, adding them to an already volatile mix is like tossing a lit match into a gas leak. You're not only jeopardising your emotional well-being; you're gambling with your children's emotional futures. The scars inflicted now can haunt them for the rest of their lives.

Now, let's talk about the 'getting' versus 'giving' dynamic in relationships. Far too many people enter a relationship focusing solely on what they can extract. But the real foundation? It's what you contribute: love, trust, support, and open, honest communication. This is why I'm penning a book; to guide you through this intricate emotional landscape, to reduce the risk of losing all that you've worked for.

Communication, or the lack of it, is often the silent assassin in relationships. Many couples naively assume that tying the knot will magically resolve their issues. Spoiler alert: it doesn't. If you're deluded enough to think that adding more responsibilities like children or a mortgage will bring stability, you're setting yourself up for failure.

I've had my share of 'interesting' relational escapades, each a lesson learned the hard way. Understanding the root cause is your first step to healing. But identifying the problem is just the tip of the iceberg; you need actionable, practical solutions to turn the ship around. And that's where I come in. With years of experience in this field, I can guide you through this intricate maze of human emotions and behavioural patterns.

So, if you're aged 35 and up, accomplished in your career but teetering on the edge with a relationship in dire straits, listen closely: I get it. The stakes are sky-high, and the fallout—both emotional and financial—of a divorce can be ruinous. But you don't have to travel this path alone. There's a light at the end of this dark tunnel—a pathway to a more resilient, fulfilling relationship.

Stick with me. Together, we can transform these stumbling blocks into stepping stones, creating a life you'll be proud to live and a legacy that will make your children proud.

"The Tipping Point: When Your Relationship Hangs in the Balance"

The Ripple Effect: Not Just About You, Mate

Gentlemen, when the pressure mounts, it's not just you who's feeling the heat. Your health starts to nosedive. Stress hormones mess with your sleep, and you find yourself diving into junk food like there's no tomorrow. Remember walking into an empty room with nothing but bare floors? That same chilling emptiness seeps into every facet of your life, from your social interactions to your self-esteem. You start snapping at colleagues, withdrawing from friends, and becoming a stranger even to yourself. You're not living; you're merely existing.

The Real Heartbreak: Losing What Matters Most

But let's talk about the true tragedy here—the loss of intimacy and the emotional rift that widens each day. Picture this: You used to have quiet dinners, meaningful conversations, and real emotional exchange. Now, the table's gone cold, the touch is absent, and the connection is lost. Imagine walking into your home only to find your wife has packed her bags for another solo trip. That's not just loneliness; that's abandonment, and it's a glaring warning sign.

Own Your Part: It Takes Two to Tango

It's all too easy to point fingers, to lay the blame solely on your partner. But let's get one thing straight: this is a partnership, not a solo act. Owning your part doesn't mean accepting all the blame; it means acknowledging that you, too, have the power to turn things around. Are you ignoring her needs? Shutting down conversations? Escaping into work? Recognise your role and take the reins; your relationship's fate isn't just in her hands.

Breaking the Loop: Your Choices Matter

Life might be a series of routines, but you're not a robot programmed to repeat the same mistakes. Notice your wife acting differently? Being overly protective of her mobile phone? That's a red flag, mate. The choice is yours—ignore it and perpetuate the cycle, or address the issue and break the loop. It could be as simple as choosing to listen instead of going on the defensive, or as monumental as seeking professional help, something you've been conveniently avoiding.

The Kids Feel It Too: Don't Underestimate Their Intuition

We've talked a lot about you, but remember, the home you're breaking or making affects your kids too. Don't underestimate their intuition; they're not blind to the tension. They sense the discord, and it shapes their understanding of relationships and family. Do you want to teach them that love is a battlefield, or a sanctuary?

Your Toolkit: You've Got What It Takes

Listen, you're not stranded without options. You've got a toolkit of resources—books, therapy, support groups. Don't discount what's out there to help you navigate through these turbulent waters. Take that first step; grab that lifeline, my contact details are at the end of this chapter.

Your Legacy: What Will You Leave Behind?

Here's the kicker. Time's ticking, and you've got a choice to make. What story do you want to tell? What legacy will you leave for your children? Will it be a tale of a broken home, filled with tension and regret? Or will it be a story of resilience, of a man who faced the abyss and pulled himself and his family back from the edge?

The clock's ticking, mate. Make your choice, not just for you, but for everyone who's a part of your world.

"Navigating the Storm: Your Lifeline to Reviving a Sinking Relationship"

HELP: Your SOS Call Answered

You might feel like you're aboard a sinking ship right now, watching as your relationship takes on water. The storm's howling, and you're grappling with how to plug the leaks. But hold on, mate. What if I told you there's an island of hope on the horizon? A sanctuary where you can repair the holes in your relationship and set sail toward smoother seas?

The Blueprint: Understanding Social Conditioning

Let's face it, many issues you're wrestling with aren't solely your fault or your partner's. According to Morris Massey, from the time of conception until about age seven, we're like sponges. We soak up our environment, mimic behaviours, adopt beliefs, and store life experiences through our senses. This is what we call 'social conditioning,' and it's the blueprint for how we act and react in relationships as adults. This is stuff that's been imprinted on us, like the grooves on a vinyl record.

The Underlying Causes: It's Not Just About the Trash

So, when your partner forgets to take out the trash or snaps over something trivial, it's not necessarily a sign of laziness or a bad temper. These could be learned behaviours, ingrained deeply in their unconscious mind. And let's be real; you've got your own quirks contributing to the tension too.

The Silver Lining: Change is Possible

But here's the lifeline. These behaviours are not etched in stone. The human mind is more like clay—moldable and capable of change. Recognizing there's a problem is the first step. Being willing to work on it? That's when change shifts from possible to probable.

The How: Digging Deep into the Unconscious Mind

You may have been wondering, how do you change something that's so deeply rooted? The answer lies in techniques that delve into the unconscious mind. That's where all these behaviours and beliefs are stashed away, like old files in a cabinet. You can pull them out, scrutinise them, and then replace them with healthier behaviours. And guess what? This transformation is often quicker and easier than you'd think.

The Reality: Communication Without Clash

Imagine a life where you communicate without constant bickering, love without conditions, and coexist without that nagging tension. It's not fantasy; it's within reach. And you don't have to go it alone. There are books, workshops, and experts ready to guide you through this maze.

Your Power: The Choice is Yours

Everyone's doing the best they can with what they've learned. But now, as an adult, you have the power to choose. You can stick with what you know, even if it's causing pain, or you can choose a different path. A path that leads to change, to healing, and to a healthier relationship.

The Lifeline: Help Is a Decision Away

If you're tired of that sinking feeling, take heart. Your lifeline is closer than you think. All you have to do is make the conscious decision to reach for it. The help you need is out there, armed with the tools you need to navigate through the storm and into calmer waters.

"Your Lighthouse: Real Stories of Transformation and Triumph"

Since 2004, I've had the privilege to be a guiding light for hundreds seeking to change their lives, and I can do the same for you. Let me spotlight some real-life stories that echo the miraculous transformations I've witnessed. These aren't just anecdotes; they're proof of what's possible.

The Emotional Vault: Ted and Martha's Journey

First in the spotlight are Ted and Martha (names changed for privacy). Imagine a couple so disconnected they lived under separate roofs. Ted was a man of few words, an emotional Fort Knox, while Martha was a fountain of feelings. It was like trying to mix oil and water. Their emotional mismatch built a resentment so thick, you could cut it with a knife. But they took a shot at change and walked through my door. After peeling off the layers in several impactful sessions, Ted found the key to his emotional vault, and Martha learned the language to understand him. They didn't just halt their trip to the divorce court; they made a U-turn back to family life, ready to embrace their children as a united front.

From Tinderbox to Harmony: Suzy and Peter's Transformation

Next, meet Suzy and Peter, a couple that was a spark away from a wildfire of arguments. Their relationship score was a measly 2/10. Yeah, that low. But a single joint session and individual follow-ups shot that score up to a respectable 7/10. Peter's bottled-up anger? We uncorked it safely, rebuilding trust that had eroded over time. A few powerful sessions were all they needed to reboot their love life.

Overcoming a Decade of Anxiety: Jan and Rob's Breakthrough

Don't overlook Jan and Rob. Rob was shackled by anxiety so severe it felt like an invisible prison. He had been in this emotional lockdown for over a decade. Just three sessions was all it took to pick the lock. We dived into the depths of his unconscious mind and unearthed a teenage fear that had grown into a monstrous anxiety. Rob was freed, and their relationship breathed a sigh of relief.

From Broken Communication to Wedding Bells: John and Jane's Love Story

And what about John and Jane? Their love was strong, but their communication was fractured, like a radio signalled that kept cutting out. They were on the verge of saying goodbye but after just two sessions with me, they found their turning point. Fast forward 16 months, and guess what? They're not signing off; they're ringing wedding bells.

The Underlying Message: Life is What You Make It

I want to hammer this home: we're all doing the best we can with the hand we've been dealt. But here's the kicker: you have the power to reshuffle that deck. It's not about the cards you were dealt; it's how you play them that counts.

Your Guiding Light: The Journey Ahead

In each of these transformational stories, I've been the lighthouse in the storm, showing people how to navigate treacherous waters to reach safer shores. Now, I offer you the same guiding light. If these remarkable people could turn their lives and relationships around, why can't you? You're not sailing through this storm alone. I'm here, ready to be your beacon, leading you toward a life of love, happiness, and the well-being you deserve.

"The Crossroads: A Call to Transform Your Tomorrow, today"

Decision Time: Your First Step Toward a Better Life

If you are still reading this, you have already taken the most crucial step. You've signaled that you're not just curious but committed to shifting your life from a roller coaster of emotional ups and downs to a smoother ride filled with happiness and peace. Congrats! Acknowledging the need for change is half the battle won. Now, it's time to put that desire into action.

You're Worth It: The Power of Self-Belief

Here's a hard truth that's also a beautiful one: You are extraordinary. You deserve love, happiness, and all the fantastic things life can offer. This isn't some motivational mumbo jumbo; it's the stone-cold truth. Your best life isn't a fantasy; it's a reality waiting for you to step into it.

Your Invitation to Change: A Choice That Echoes

I'm extending an invitation, my friend. Reach out. Do it for yourself. Do it out of love and respect for your family. Do it because there's a spectacular life filled with joy, love, and satisfaction hiding just around the corner. This isn't about 'maybe' or 'someday.' It's about right now. The payoffs are way bigger than you can even imagine.

The Clock is Ticking: Can You Afford Not To?

"I'm too busy," you might say. "My calendar's jam-packed." I get it. Life has a habit of getting in the way. But let me ask you: Can you afford NOT to take this step? What's the real cost of inaction? How many sunsets, laughter-filled dinners, and loving moments will you let slip by? Your time is precious, yes, but so is your happiness.

No-Risk Opportunity: Your Free 'Relationship Assessment'

To make this as simple as possible, I've opened up specific time slots just for you—a Free **30-minute 'Relationship Assessment**.' No strings attached. It's your chance to taste the transformation that awaits. To grab this opportunity, all you have to do is shoot an email to: *help@happycouple.au* with **'MAB-Free-Session-Offer**' in the subject line. This is your moment. Don't let it slip through your fingers.

Wise Words to Ponder

"If you want to change some things in your life, you have to change some things in your life." - Jim Rohn

"If it's going to be, it's up to me." - Robert Schuller

These are not just words; they're principles that can guide your life. They underscore the power of choice and action.

Your Life, Your Choice

Your life is like an unfolding book, and the pen is firmly in your grip. What will you write? A story filled with missed opportunities, or a tale of bravery, initiative, and transformation? You stand at a crossroads. One path offers more of the unfulfilling same, while the other leads to a life you can't wait to wake up for. The crucial choice is yours alone to make. The stage is ready, a better life waits on the horizon. The moment for action is now.

Chapter 5

From Reviews to Revenue: Turn Your Reviews into a Goldmine in 3 Steps

Scott Baker
Creator of Reviewology and RevGenHub.com Healer

About The Author: Scott Baker

Scott Baker is the creator of Reviewology and a qualified reviewologist, specializing in the brain science behind why people buy.

With 30 years of experience in sales and marketing, Scott understands the challenges business owners face in standing out in a crowded market. He believes in the power of authentic connections and promoting a brand through the people who have used and loved it.

Scott is also the co-creator of RevGenHub.com, a cutting-edge tool that combines science with technology, allowing business owners to effectively convey their unique message in the digital landscape. He blends his expertise in sales and marketing with the latest technology to help clients navigate the complex digital world.

As an Authentic Connection Expert, Scott is committed to helping businesses build genuine relationships, establish authentic branding, and deeply connect with their target audience. He believes that every business owner deserves to be acknowledged and celebrated for their passion and expertise.

By working with Scott, clients can expect increased customer trust and loyalty, leading to enhanced referrals and business growth. He guides clients through the complexities of the digital landscape, ensuring their unique voice is heard and appreciated.

Scott's goal is to help clients create a deeply resonant brand message that authentically reflects their values and passions.

If you're a business owner or entrepreneur looking to stand out in a crowded market, Scott Baker is the expert you need. With his expertise, guidance, and passion for authentic connection, he can help you build a brand that deeply resonates with your audience and creates a lasting impact.

Don't let fear or technological obstacles hold you back. Trust Scott Baker to help you unleash the power of authenticity and take your brand to new heights.

From Reviews to Revenue: Turn Your Reviews into a Goldmine in 4 Steps

- *93% of consumers read online reviews before making a purchase decision. [BrightLocal, 2023]*
- *Displaying reviews can increase conversion rates by 270%. (Spiegel Research Center)*
- *63% of consumers trust search engines, while 70% trust online reviews. (The Edelman Trust Barometer)*

Imagine you are walking down the street, and you see two restaurants.

One restaurant has a long line of people waiting outside, and the other restaurant is empty.

Which restaurant would you choose to eat at?

Most people would choose the restaurant with the long line, because they assume that it must be good if so many people are willing to wait to eat there.

This is because social proof plays a crucial role in our decision-making process.

We are more likely to choose products or services that are popular and well-regarded by others.

The same principle applies to customer reviews and testimonials. When potential customers see that a business has a lot of positive reviews, they are more likely to trust that business and make a purchase.

In fact, a recent study by BrightLocal found that 93% of consumers read online reviews before making a purchase decision.

This means that customer reviews are one of the most important factors that influence consumer behaviour.

To harness the power of reviews and turn positive feedback into increased revenue, businesses must first take the crucial initial step of discovering the hidden gems within their reviews.

Step 1: Discover the Hidden Gems Within Your Reviews

In today's digital age, social proof has become an essential tool for businesses and individuals looking to build trust and credibility.

It refers to the psychological phenomenon where people are more likely to do something if they see others doing it.

Customer reviews and testimonials are a key form of social proof, as they serve as a signal to potential customers that your products or services are high quality and trustworthy.

Here are just a few examples of how businesses are using social proof to their advantage:

- Amazon: Amazon prominently displays customer reviews on its product pages. This is a key factor in Amazon's success, as it helps to build trust with potential customers and increase sales.
- Airbnb: Airbnb allows guests to leave reviews of their hosts. This helps build trust between guests and hosts and encourages people to book Airbnb listings.
- LinkedIn: LinkedIn allows users to endorse each other for their skills and experience. This is a great way for professionals to build their social proof and attract potential employers and clients.

How Businesses Can Use Social Proof to Increase Website Traffic, Generate Leads, and Boost Sales

Increase website traffic

- Display customer reviews and testimonials prominently on your website homepage. This will show potential visitors that your products or services are well-regarded by others and encourage them to stay on your website and learn more.
- Include social sharing buttons on your website so that visitors can easily share your content with their followers. This is a great way to spread the word about your business and attract new visitors to your website.

Generate leads

- Offer gated content, such as white papers, ebooks, and webinars, in exchange for visitors' contact information. This is a great way to collect leads from potential customers who are interested in what you have to offer.
- Use social proof to promote your lead generation offers. For example, you could highlight the number of people who have already downloaded your white paper or registered for your webinar.
- Run paid social media ads that target your ideal audience with your lead generation offers.

Boost sales

- Include social proof on your product pages, such as customer reviews, star ratings, and the number of people who have purchased the product. This will help to reassure potential customers they are making a good purchase decision.
- Use social proof in your email marketing campaigns. For example, you could include a testimonial from a satisfied customer in your email newsletter.
- Run social media ads that promote your products or services and highlight your social proof.

- *A product with hundreds of positive reviews on Amazon is more likely to be seen as high quality and trustworthy than a product with no reviews or lots of negative reviews.*
- *A company with a strong social media presence and a large number of followers is more likely to be seen as credible and legitimate than a company with a weak social media presence.*
- *A person with a LinkedIn profile that includes endorsements from former colleagues and clients is more likely to be seen as qualified and experienced than a person with a blank LinkedIn profile.*

When potential customers see that a business or individual has a lot of positive social proof, they are more likely to trust that business or individual and make a purchase or hire them.

The good news is that you likely already have a wealth of social proof lurking within your reach.

Customer reviews and testimonials, social media followers, and endorsements from others are all valuable forms of social proof.

By uncovering these hidden gems and understanding their impact, you can start to leverage your social proof to build trust and credibility and achieve your goals.

Step 2: Leverage Your Reviews for Maximum Impact

Let's delve deeper into the strategies and techniques you can employ to leverage your reviews for maximum impact.

Identifying key themes and messages in reviews

The first step in leveraging your reviews is to identify the common themes and messages that emerge from your customers' feedback.

By closely examining the language and sentiments expressed in your reviews, you can uncover the unique selling points that your customers value most.

These key themes serve as the foundation for crafting a compelling brand image that aligns with what your customers want and expect from you.

Here are some tips on how to identify key themes and messages in reviews:

- Use keyword analysis to identify common words and phrases used in your reviews. This can be done using a variety of tools, such as Google Keyword Planner or WordStream Keyword Tool.
- Use sentiment analysis to identify the overall sentiment of your reviews. This can be done using a variety of tools, such as Google Cloud Natural Language API or Amazon Comprehend.
- Read through your reviews carefully and look for patterns and trends. What are the things your customers like and dislike most about your products or services? What are the common benefits they mention?
- Talk to your customers directly. Ask them what they appreciate most about your business and what you could do better.
- Take a peek at what reviews your competitors are getting and look for any gaps that may be obvious.

Crafting a compelling brand image that aligns with customer sentiments

Once you have identified the key themes and messages in your reviews, you can use them to craft a compelling brand image that aligns with customer sentiments. Here are some tips:

- Use your reviews to develop a clear and concise value proposition. What makes your business unique and valuable to your customers?

- Highlight the benefits your customers value most. What problems does your business solve for your customers? What needs does it meet?
- Use your reviews to create a relatable and trustworthy brand voice. Let your customers' voices shine through in your marketing materials.
- Be authentic and genuine. Customers can spot a fake from a mile away, so make sure your brand image is true to who you are and what your business stands for.

Here are some examples of how businesses are crafting compelling brand images that align with customer sentiments:

- Nike: Nike's brand image is all about empowering athletes and helping them achieve their goals. This is reflected in their marketing materials, which often feature inspiring stories and testimonials from real athletes.
- Apple: Apple's brand image is all about innovation and simplicity. This is reflected in their product design, marketing materials, and even their retail stores.
- Tesla: Tesla's brand image is all about sustainability and the future of transportation. This is reflected in their products, which are electric and environmentally friendly.

Showcasing your reviews across various marketing channels

To amplify the reach of your positive reviews, consider featuring them on your website homepage, creating a dedicated testimonial page, or incorporating them into your email marketing campaigns.

You can also share snippets of your positive reviews on your social media platforms, accompanied by eye-catching visuals or testimonials from satisfied customers.

Encourage your followers to share their own experiences and reviews, further expanding the reach and impact of your social proof.

By strategically placing your reviews where your target audience can see them, you are increasing the chances of capturing their attention and building trust in your brand.

However, simply showcasing your reviews is not enough.

To truly harness the power of your social proof, you need to go beyond surface-level exposure.

In Step 3, we will explore how you can repurpose your social proof in more creative and engaging ways to captivate and engage your target audience.

We'll discuss the creation of attention-grabbing visuals that highlight your best reviews, as well as how to strategically integrate your social proof into your marketing materials.

Step 3: Repurpose Your Social Proof to Supercharge Your Success

Now that we have explored the importance of social proof and its role in building trust and credibility, let's dive deeper into how you can repurpose it to boost your success.

Create attention-grabbing visuals

Visuals are a powerful way to capture attention and communicate your message effectively.

Consider creating eye-catching graphics that highlight your best reviews and testimonials.

These visuals can be shared on your website, social media platforms, and even in printed materials such as brochures or business cards.

Here are a few specific examples of how you can use visuals to repurpose your social proof:

1. Create a carousel post on Instagram that features snippets of your best reviews.
2. Design a series of infographics that highlight the key benefits that your customers value most.
3. Create a short video that features customer testimonials and showcases the benefits of your products or services.
4. Use images of your customers using and enjoying your products or services, accompanied by positive reviews.

Strategically integrate your social proof

Rather than simply displaying your testimonials on a web page, think about integrating them seamlessly into your overall marketing strategy. This will help you to reinforce the trust and credibility you have built with your target audience.

Here are a few specific examples of how you can strategically integrate your social proof into your marketing materials:

- Include snippets of positive reviews in the header or footer of your website.
- Incorporate testimonials into the design of your email newsletters.
- Add a testimonial section to your product pages or landing pages.
- Use customer reviews and testimonials in your social media posts and ads.
- Create a case study that features a customer's success story and testimonial.

Captivate your target audience

Your social proof is not just a static asset; it can be used to engage your target audience and build relationships with potential customers.

Consider using your social proof as a starting point for conversations and storytelling. Here's how:

- Ask your social media followers to share their own experiences and opinions related to the topics discussed in your reviews.
- Host a live Q&A session where you answer questions from your audience and share customer testimonials.
- Create a blog post or series of blog posts that feature customer stories and testimonials.
- Run a contest or giveaway where people are encouraged to share their reviews of your products or services.
- Partner with influencers to share their experiences with your products or services and provide their testimonials.

By repurposing your social proof in creative and engaging ways, you can effectively captivate your target audience and build stronger relationships with potential customers.

Handling negative feedback

Negative feedback can be daunting, but it is important to remember that it is a normal part of doing business. In fact, how you handle negative feedback can be just as important as how you showcase your positive feedback.

Here are some tips on how to handle negative feedback:

- Respond promptly and professionally. Acknowledge the customer's feedback and apologise for any inconvenience or frustration they may have experienced.

- Take the feedback seriously and investigate the issue. Once you have a better understanding of the situation, you can take steps to resolve it and address the customer's concerns.
- Be proactive and transparent. Let the customer know what you are doing to resolve the issue and keep them updated on your progress.
- Offer the customer a platform to share their feedback directly with you. This could be through a customer satisfaction survey, feedback form, or live chat feature. By providing customers with a way to share their feedback directly with you, you can demonstrate your commitment to listening to your customers and improving your business.
- Negative Reviews have the ability to be the most viewed marketing you create so make sure your responses take this into consideration. If you have hundreds of reviews and five negative ones, you can be sure the negative ones and your responses will be read the most.

Ensuring authenticity

It is important to ensure that your testimonials are genuine and that you have obtained proper consent from customers before sharing them.

Here are some tips on how to ensure the authenticity of your social proof:

- Only use testimonials from real customers. Do not fabricate testimonials or use quotes from celebrities or other public figures without their permission.
- Include customer names and photos with testimonials. This will help to build trust and credibility with potential customers.
- Use a variety of testimonials from different customers. This will show that your positive feedback is not just coming from a small group of people.
- Be transparent about how you collect and use testimonials. Let customers know how you use their feedback and how they can opt out if they do not want their testimonials to be used.

By following these tips, you can handle negative feedback professionally, ensure the authenticity of your social proof, and leverage the power of social proof to grow your business.

Step 4:Automate Your Testimonial Campaign and Watch Your Sales Soar

Once you have repurposed your social proof to create attention-grabbing visuals and strategically integrate it into your marketing materials, you can take things to the next level by automating your testimonial campaign.

This will allow you to collect and showcase testimonials from your customers at scale.

Case Studies

One of my clients, a world-renowned business coach, was able to generate $204,000 in sales in just six weeks using a testimonial campaign.

The campaign was so successful that we ran additional video testimonial campaigns using the testimonials generated from the first campaign.

The second campaign produced an impressive $564,000 in sales over 4 months.

All the campaigns were automated, making them very easy to manage and scale.

Case Study 1: Automated Video Testimonial Campaign

Metric	Value
Revenue	$204,000
Testimonials collected	70 video testimonials
Content generated	350 minutes user generated marketing content
Campaign Duration	6 weeks

*** 28% of clients who did a video testimony purchased the program*

Case Study 2: Automated Video Testimonial Campaign

Metric	Value
Revenue	$564,00
Testimonials collected	215 video testimonials
Content generated	1000 minutes user generated marketing content
Campaign Duration	4 months

Another client, a publicly listed retail company, has been working with me for about 18 months.

They have received over 1,000 Google reviews, seen a 173% increase in online contacts (email/phone inquiries), and experienced a 27% increase in their share price.

Case Study 3: Automated Google Review Campaign

Metric	Value
Reviews collected	1000+ Google Reviews
Increased contacts	173% increase
Increased share price	27% increase
Campaign duration	18 months

How to Automate Your Testimonial Campaign to Generate Revenue

1. Choose a testimonial automation platform. There are several different platforms available, so it is important to choose one that is right for your needs. Consider factors such as price, features, and ease of use.
2. Create a testimonial landing page. This is a dedicated page on your website where customers can submit their testimonials. Be sure to include persuasive copy and social proof elements on the page to encourage customers to leave testimonials.
3. Segment your customers and send targeted testimonial requests. For example, you could send different testimonial requests to new customers, existing customers, and high-value customers.
4. Use a testimonial automation platform to automatically capture and moderate testimonials. This will save you time and allow you to scale your testimonial campaign.
5. Showcase your testimonials prominently on your website and in your marketing materials. This will help you to build trust and credibility with potential customers.

By automating your testimonial campaign, you can collect and showcase testimonials from your customers at scale. This will help you to boost your sales, attract dream clients, establish preeminent authority, and skyrocket your SEO performance.

Activate Your Social Proof: Generate Leads, Boost Sales, and Skyrocket Your Business

Make your business go viral with the power of social proof!

Unlock your hidden success assets and achieve unparalleled achievements by activating your social proof.

Follow the four steps to skyrocketing your business:

Step 1: Identify your hidden gems. These are the positive reviews and testimonials you've already received from customers.

These gems can be found on your website, Google reviews, social media, and other online platforms.

Step 2: Leverage your reviews for maximum impact. Craft a compelling brand image that aligns with your customers' sentiments and showcase your reviews across various marketing channels.

Step 3: Repurpose your social proof to supercharge your success. Transform your best reviews into attention-grabbing visuals to integrate into your marketing materials, such as your website landing pages, social media, and email campaigns.

Step 4: Automate your testimonial campaign and watch your sales soar.

Collect and showcase testimonials at scale to boost sales, attract dream clients, establish preeminent authority, and skyrocket your SEO performance.

The time has come to seize the opportunity before you and make your dreams a reality.

Your journey towards success begins now.

Chapter 6

Climbing The Property Ladder: From Property Investor to Property Developer

Rob Flux
Founder of Property Developer Network and Development Sites Australia

About The Author: Rob Flux

Rob Flux is a passionate educator and the driving force behind Property Developer Network, Development Sites Australia, and a founding board member of National Property Data.

He leads the largest national network of property developers, uniting over 23,000 Australians with a shared goal of achieving financial freedom through property development.

Rob's personal mission is to empower 1,000 individuals to attain financial freedom by 2030. To achieve this, he employs a comprehensive strategy that includes monthly networking events in major cities, online Facebook communities, live training sessions, a development sites platform, and a 12-month education program for novice and aspiring property developers.

Starting with just five friends gathered around his kitchen table, Rob's Property Developer Network has grown into the largest Property Networking group in Australia since its inception in August 2012.

It now operates in four major cities, hosting monthly events that share industry expertise, showcase real deals within the community, and offer a unique masterminding experience, recreating the original kitchen table experience

Rob's latest ventures include Development Sites Australia which addresses common frustrations in property dealings by providing free site assessments and instant matches with qualified buyers, all at no cost to homeowners and National Property Data, a powerful property data, marketing, and sales platform offering 40 years of Australian property insights, trusted by property developers, real estate agents, valuers and investors.

Rob is renowned for launching the property development careers of thousands of community members, with hundreds having already transitioned to full-time developers.

His guiding philosophy emphasizes collective problem-solving in property development, recognizing the strength of collaboration in overcoming challenges.

★★★

In this chapter, my intent is to provide the reader with clear, actionable advice on how to transition from property investment to property development, demystifying complex topics to make them accessible to all, and highlighting the unique challenges and opportunities in each field.

At the end of the chapter, I will also be giving you to opportunity to access my FREE COURSE - The 7 Step Formula to Financial Freedom.

My journey through property development has been anything but ordinary. I bought my first house at the tender age of 18, fueled by a childhood marked by hardship and resilience.

Growing up in Darwin, my family's life was turned upside down by Cyclone Tracy in 1974, leaving us with nothing but the remnants of a brand new house.

For five long years, I called a caravan under the floorboards of our destroyed home my sanctuary, showering behind a corrugated iron curtain and living with the constant reminder of our financial distress.

My parents were uninsured. Having lost their property in the cyclone they were determined to rebuild, despite the financial strain. Witnessing their struggles, I vowed to carve a different path for myself. So, at 18, impetuous but driven, I took a bold step: I bought my family home from my parents, freeing them from financial turmoil and setting the stage for my future.

But this was no ordinary teenage rebellion. As a second-year apprentice earning just $4 an hour, I took on financial responsibilities beyond my years, all while continuing to support my parents. Inspired by investment guru Jan Summers, I dove headfirst into the world of property investment, unknowingly timing the market to perfection and securing a windfall with my first investment property at 21. By 24, I owned my first home outright... in all honesty, it was a fluke. I just timed the market well, and I had many hard lessons still to learn.

But success came at a cost. My journey was riddled with financial roadblocks and glass ceilings in not being able to come up with deposits, or being unable to service debt to buy my next deal, slowing down my investment journey. Despite accumulating assets, it took 20 years to achieve financial freedom - only to have it stripped away by a divorce at 37.

Starting from scratch, I found myself at a crossroads, grappling with depression and contemplating my next move. Property development beckoned, promising a way to manufacture profits and regain control.... But where to start?

I attended seminar after seminar from educators promising me quick riches from the property development process, only to be let down with the lack of detail in what they presented, and $120k out of pocket in the process.

I knew there had to be a better way. Upon reading the Napoleon Hill book "Think & Grow Rich", I discovered the power of the mastermind process. Armed with a newfound sense of purpose and a pay-it-forward mentality, I gathered a group of like-minded friends around my kitchen table, determined to master the art of property development together.

As each mate invited another mate, our community grew into what is now the largest property networking group in the country - Property Developer Network.

Oh - and for the record, I made it out in 6 years the second time around :)

Common Pitfalls of Property Investing

For many Australians, property investment holds the promise of building wealth and creating a foundation for financial stability.

However, this journey is fraught with pitfalls that can stymie even the most diligent investor.

Property investment is a long-term play, demanding both time and financial resources.

Let's take Louis for example.

He's a great guy; really put his all into property investment. He and his wife took the plunge and bought their first property with dreams of climbing the property ladder to financial freedom.

And that's fantastic - it's a big step and I commend them for it.

But here's the thing. After that initial purchase, they found themselves in a bit of a standstill.

They owned a property, sure, but what next?

They were stuck in a cycle of waiting, hoping for their property's value to shoot up.

Now, their property was appreciating in value, don't get me wrong. But it was a slow process.

Louis and his wife were caught in what I call the "equity trap."

Their property's value was creeping up, but not enough to leverage and reinvest. Their journey had plateaued.

You see, they were moving an inch when they had the potential to move a mile.

They'd taken the first steps towards building wealth, but were now stuck.

And Louis isn't the only one. This is a common story in property investment, and it's an important one. It's a reminder that buying property is just one piece of the financial puzzle.

In fact, statistically speaking, of the 2.1 million property investors in Australia, only 10% of them ever manage to accumulate more than 2 properties because they keep hitting glass ceilings of equity and serviceability, and so very few ever make it out. In fact, only 4% of all Property Investors ever make it to even purchasing 4 or more properties, let alone being able to own them outright so that they are generating enough passive income to support their Financial Freedom.

Financial Freedom and Rob's Philosophy

Property development presents a more direct route to financial independence, placing the reins firmly in your hands. Trust me, it took me 20 years doing it with property investing, and only 6 years with property development. Knowing what I know now, I could do it again in 3 years if I needed too.

Unlike traditional property investment, which relies on market forces and long-term appreciation, property development is a proactive journey.

It's a journey where your effort, skills, and strategic planning directly translate into value creation and financial growth.

At the heart of property development is the ability to manufacture profit in any market, up, down or sideways.

This is achieved not by waiting for market conditions to favour you, but by actively transforming properties and realising their full potential.

This unique approach allows for a faster accumulation of wealth, providing a more direct and immediate route to financial independence.

What does financial freedom truly mean?

Let me first tell you what it's not.... It's not the flashy car, and it's not the big house, or owning a lear jet. It's about taking control of your destiny and creating stock at a wholesale price, rather than a retail price as you would as a Property Investor.

It's about breaking free from the constraints of the nine-to-five, securing your financial future, and reclaiming time for yourself and your loved ones.

It's about having enough passive income to cover your living and leisure expenses, freeing you from the need to work.

This newfound freedom is the real promise of property development; it grants you the power to choose how you spend your time, whether that's pursuing further wealth, spending quality time with family, or travelling the world.

My Approach

My unique approach to building wealth combines both the foresight of a property investor with the ingenuity of a property developer.

As property developers, we don't just aim to accumulate properties; we strive to create value and generate passive income.

We navigate a careful balance, selling enough property to offset debt while retaining assets that continue to generate income.

This approach not only maximises profit but also ensures a sustainable and prosperous financial future.

What makes this approach so effective?

It lies in the unique financial mechanics of property development.

The deposit and subsequent property value are generated through the development process itself, eliminating the need for substantial upfront savings.

This means that, with a sufficiently large project, the resulting debt can be minimal or even nonexistent, leaving you with a property that is fully paid off and generating positive cash flow.

This strategy not only fast-tracks your journey to financial independence but also insulates you from common financial pitfalls.

With little to no debt, you are immune to fluctuating interest rates, and inflation becomes an ally rather than an adversary.

As rents naturally increase over time, your income rises while your expenses remain static, resulting in an ever-growing passive income stream.

Introduction to Property Development

Property development isn't just about waiting for things to happen; it's about making things happen.

Think of it this way: we're not just buying properties; we're creating them. And in doing so, we're building up our financial future.

Imagine having properties that don't just cost you money, but make you money, week in and week out. That's the power of property development.

Now, I know what you might be thinking – this sounds risky. And you're not wrong. Property development has its risks.

But as the wise Warren Buffett says, "Risk comes from not knowing what you're doing."

And that's what we're here to tackle. It's the fear of the unknown that stops many from ever starting.

How much money is needed to get started?

A common misconception is thinking you need a ton of money to start in property development.

But here's the truth: it's not about how much money you have, it's about how well you use it. It's a different game than property investing, and it requires a different mindset.

It's all about controlling the property, not owning it like we have been tought to think. In fact there are 7 ways that we call "No & Low Money Down" strategies that allow you to control a property and profit from the property development process that alow you to defer, or sometimes avoid altogether many of the costs in the deal allowing you to make money even when starting with not much at all.

So, let's treat property development like a career. Let's learn the ins and outs, step by step, just like an apprenticeship.

Scalable Development Strategies

The first step in your property development journey is choosing your strategy. Whilst there are hundreds of development strategies out there, there are only two strategies with scalable paths: subdivisions and multi-residential developments, including townhouses or units.

By scalable, I mean starting with smaller projects that let you gradually build the essential skills, confidence, and financial stability needed to transition to larger deals, leveraging the skills and lessons learnt from the previous project as you increase your deal size.

Whether you choose subdivisions and multi-residential developments, the idea is to start small, learning and honing your skills on more manageable projects.

As you progress, the temptation to shift strategies might arise, with bright-shiny-object-itis causing you to jump strategies looking for quicker wins.

However, the power of consistency cannot be overstated. By sticking to one proven strategy, you create a solid foundation, allowing for incremental growth and mastery.

The goal here is to evolve within your chosen path, scaling up in deal size and complexity while maintaining a steadfast approach.

This consistency not only sharpens your expertise but also fortifies your financial position, paving the way for sustained success in property development.

Market Research

Now, market research might sound fancy, but it's really just about doing your homework. You've got to dig deep and really get to know the ins and outs of different suburbs.

I'm talking about places that are just ripe for the picking, where our specific deal will thrive.

This isn't just about finding a good suburb; it's about finding the RIGHT suburb for our unique deal.

Now, here's where we can really play it smart. There's no need to reinvent the wheel. Other people have walked this path before us..

Look for suburbs where others have successfully executed similar deals. These are the locations where similar projects have thrived, ensuring there's enough demand and proven profitability.

If there's a proven track record of success in a particular area, that's a giant neon sign pointing us in the right direction.
Now, let's talk about demand.

We've got to ensure that by the time our development is ready to hit the market, people are going to be lining up around the block.

Are we looking at an area on the up? Are businesses moving in? Are there schools and amenities that draw folks into the suburb?

We want our development to be the answer to what the market is demanding.

We're playing the long game. We need to anticipate the future and ensure that the demand we're seeing today is going to stick around.

Scaling Your Projects

Now, it's time to roll up our sleeves and use what we've learned to make our next projects even better. Remember, every project, big or small, is a chance to learn and grow.

It's crucial to reflect on and leverage lessons learned from previous projects.

Examine what went well and what could have been done differently. This introspective process will serve as a foundation for enhancing future projects.

Begin by stepping up the deal size incrementally.

If your first project involved developing two units, aim for four in your next venture, then six, and so on.

This strategic increase not only allows you to manage risks but also enables you to apply the lessons learned from smaller deals to larger ones.

Manufacturing Profits & Keeping Stock

Our ultimate goal is retaining properties for passive income. Not just rental income, but positively geared 'passive income'.

But there's a catch.... And I see many in my community fall for it on a daily basis. We have all been indoctrinated to keep every property we ever purchase. But keeping stock too early in the process can be a massive handbrake to your journey. It will tie up your cash resources and leave you with a massive debt, meaning that in periods of high interest rates, you could be in for a massive impact on your cashflow.

So... the obvious question is then, How & When should I be keeping my stock?

It's made possible by my 'Magic #6'.
Stick with me.

As Property Developers, we are aiming for 20% profit on costs for each individual development project.

So, lets do the maths.

If you take on a 6-pack project and each of the dwellings gets you 20% profit, then technically if I sell down 5 of them, all of the costs are paid. This means I get to keep the last one for FREE.... Plus some splash cash to have a small holiday or celebration also.

That's why the #6 is so magic....We can materialise a free property out of thin air.

Now let's say you're someone who has their processes dialled in and hits a 25% profit.

Now, you only need FIVE deals to achieve that free property.

And if you're aiming higher, like 30%, just FOUR in the project will do the trick.

See what I'm getting at?

The more profit you make per project, the quicker you're collecting properties with 100% positive cash flow.

But here is the real kicker....

That 6th one... If you never sell it, then you don't "realise" the profits from the project, so you don't pay the tax (yet), meaning that you are effectively keep 100% of the profits as stock. Now don't get me wrong, this is not a tax avoidance scheme, but rather a tax deferral scheme. At some point in the distant future you may choose to sell the property, in which case you would pay the tax then... but why would you sell it when it is 100% positively geared and paying you $25-30k passive income per year?

Oh - And now that it is owned 100% outright, you are immune to interest rate rises, your property will still grow in value with the market growing your net wealth, and rents will still go up over time, growing your cashflow... This is a cash cow that just keeps on giving.

Why This Works Every Time

The answer's simple. It's all in the maths and the method.

Begin by setting your sights on securing a solid 20% profit on each deal. As you gradually increase your ventures to encompass 6-pack projects, you'll find yourself acquiring properties outright.

Let's get this straight: they're not just any investment properties. They're FREE investment properties, all set to get you that 100% positive cash flow.

This strategy? It's one of a kind.

Now for most people, five years is enough to get ourselves financially free.

Remember, this is enough passive income to maintain your current lifestyle: i.e. putting food on the table, fueling the car, sending the kids to school...

And once you hit that milestone - The sky's the limit!

So how do we get there I hear you ask?

Well, start with the end in mind. If you know you need to do a 6-pack to keep one, then how do you start to learn how to do 6… start with a smaller version, perhaps a 4-pack. And how do you learn to do a 4-pack… do a smaller version of that, a 2-pack.

In other words, start small, learn the skills and scale up from there. Leveraging the skills from the previous project as you step up in deal size.

Introducing… The Property Development Formula

A commonsense path to building wealth

In the following pages, I will outline a commonsense path to building wealth with property development, one that's uncomplicated, low risk and one that's used by successful property developers in our community all over Australia...

And this is not just theory-based information, this is down to earth, how-to techniques that you can apply to your property developing straight away.

I've done the research through a combination of my own deals, the deals of my students, and members of our 23,000+ strong community and distilled it down to a step-by step "FORMULA" for succeeding in property development - all with people like you in mind.

Who is the Property Development Formula for?

The Property Development Formula works for:

First time developers: Even if you are just starting out - in fact it's perfect for you because you will be getting it right from the very start and laying the foundation for rapid success.

Experienced developers: It will work for you even if you have already done one or more deals.

There are many successful developers already inside The Property Developer Network and they are learning new and valuable techniques every month.

Full time employees: It will work for you even if you have a full time job and you're conducting your developments as a side hustle!

Everything I share in this book will work for you too.

Whether you're a raw newbie or a development veteran, the property development formula will accelerate your development journey (and make it a lot more fun).

Who is it NOT for?

Before we go any further, I need to be 100% honest with you:

If you're looking for yet another...

- Get Rich Quick scheme that promises millions of dollars in under 12 months...
- Or some method of preying on someone's misfortune to make money.
- Or yet another "Fad property strategy".

You know what I mean and let's just be honest: these are not solutions, they are train wrecks waiting to happen, and you KNOW they don't work.

If that's you—and I'm trusting it's not—then The Property Development Formula is really not for you. You can save yourself some time and stop reading.

The Property Development Formula is for people who are ready to stop looking for "miracles" and start doing the hard work necessary to achieve real results.

Let me be clear. It's going to require you to do some work. Property development isn't easy (nothing worthwhile is).

But if you're looking for the REAL TRUTH behind what it takes to reach your financial goals with property development, please read on. The Property Development Formula is for you.

Finances

Financial Self-Assessment - Determine how much passive income you need to pay the bills day to day & buy your time back.

Understanding your financial position also helps you to understand your challenges in how you are going to overcome the deposit to purchase, the servicability to fund the debt, and the liquid cash to run the deal.

Opportunity

5 Year Property Action Plan - Determine what opportunities will you chase starting with choosing your development strategy, starting deal size & deal trajectory to get the job done.

This is the plan that will help you to start small, learn the skills and then scale to larger deals where you will be able to keep your stock as profits. All the way you will be using the lessons learnt from the prior projects that you do along the way to get more efficient and effective on each and every deal.

Research

Suburb Selection Process - Narrow your focus to 1 council & 3 suburbs, then become an area expert. Find areas with lots of potential, & evidence others have done it before you & been profitable.

Method

Rapid Elimination Method - Throw away the dud deals fast (in just 10 minutes) so that you can look at more deals in less time.

Unlike everyone else who look for reasons to keep a deal, you will be looking for reasons to throw it away. The quicker you can thow away a dud deal, the more deals you can look at.

Under Contract

Lock in the deal - What legal documents, funding models and entity structures are needed to get the deal done.

Logistics

Project Management - Development Approvals, Building Approvals, Construction, Sales & project closeout.

Accelerate

Scale your business - Step up your deal size by following your 5 Year Property Action Plan.

Look back to Step 1 of the FORMULA "Finances" and reassess your new financial situation as you prepare to step up your deal size. Then keep on going through the rest of the 7 Steps again as you progress along your journey.

Conclusion

Property development presents a powerful path to financial freedom. By actively creating value through strategic projects, you can achieve financial independence faster than traditional investment alone.

Start small, choose a consistent strategy, and scale up gradually. Learn from others' successes, conduct thorough market research, and retain properties for pure profit.

With the right skills and mindset, you can leverage property development to create sustainable passive income.

The journey requires diligence, perseverance and a willingness to continuously learn.

But the rewards are immense, putting financial freedom firmly within your grasp. You now hold the key; it's time to unlock your potential.

How to Book Rob to Speak on Your Stage

Rob is available for a wide range of speaking engagements from small 5 minutes spots to full keynote presentations right across the country, from keynote speeches, to online webinars, interviews for radio or TV, Rob has done it all.

Some topics to consider Rob for include:

- Small Scale Property Developments
- How to invest with little to no money
- Houses of Multiple Occupancy (HMO)
- Property Development Strategies
- Mindset of being a successful Property Developer
- Resiliency in overcoming obstacles both physical and mental
- Masterminding techniques
- Growing your net worth form Zero to Hero (Twice)
- Property Investing Vs Property Developing
- How Property Developers assess sites Vs investors or emotional purchasers

Some of Rob's recent media appearances include:

- News.com.au (Interview)
- Real Estate Talk (Podcast)
- 10 Eyewitness News (Interview)
- ABC Radio (Interview)
- Australian Property Institute (Keynote Speaker)
- Property Investory Podcast (Regular guest)
- Australian Property Expo (Moderator & Keynote Speaker)

You can book Rob by reaching out to his Executive Assistance at *execassist@developernetwork.com.au* or calling 0438 225 878

BONUS FREE COURSE - 7 Step FORMULA

If you have enjoyed this chapter, then why not download my FREE - 7 Step FORMULA to Financial Freedom.

Your development path is defined in 7 Key Steps: Finances, Opportunity, Research, Method, Under Contract, Logistics, and Accelerate...

Each a crucial phase in the 5-year strategy to building lasting wealth through property development.

Let's make your property development ambitions a reality!

Join our FREE course now, and take the first step towards building your future. I can't wait to share this knowledge with you!

Chapter 7

A Risk-Free Way To Acquire A Flood Of New Buyers - Virtually Free

Pauline Martin-Brooks

Strategic Partnerships Expert, Accountability Coach & Therapist

About The Author: Pauline Martin-Brooks

Pauline Martin-Brooks is an undisputed expert in teaching people how to collaborate with their ideal partners. She's been successfully implementing this Strategic Partnerships strategy since 2003.

Pauline is the secret ingredient you can't do without. In professional circles, she's hailed as the Partnerships Queen, responsible for channeling millions of dollars in revenue. Her prowess has consistently filled events, from cozy gatherings to colossal conferences with up to 2000 attendees.

As a business mentor involved in several Australian programs for entrepreneurs, a captivating keynote speaker, and a guest webinar host, Pauline's passion lies in connecting with good-hearted individuals.

She's co-author of the international best-seller "Millionaire Mentors." This achievement is a testament to her ability to leverage the connections she's fostered through her Strategic Partnerships.

Well versed in all aspects of the partnership process, Pauline teaches everything from researching and identifying your potential partners, building rapport, delivering something of value and scaling the process through systems.

As an automation guru she loves the tech side, as a Rapid Transformational Therapist Pauline has a unique insight into self sabotage and procrastination that often plagues business owners.

With qualifications in Neuro Linguistic Programming she understands how to persuade with integrity and as one of Australia's top accountability coaches, Pauline knows how to keep her clients both motivated and on track to achieve their business growth goals.

Pauline is an Ontraport Certified Consultant and is no stranger to marketing and conversion funnels.

She works with Business Owners to help them and their teams implement projects to help scale service based businesses.

Oh, and when she's not orchestrating remarkable partnerships, you can find her dancing her heart out or soaking up the beauty of nature whenever she gets the chance!

If I could show you a way to triple or maybe even quadruple your sales in less time with more fun, would you do it?

Of course you would, but here's the thing, it takes some preparation and some courage.

I can help you with preparation and lucky for you, competence breeds confidence, so from there it's a short jump to feeling courageous!

Are you ready? Let's do this.

"So Pauline, what is this miracle business growth strategy?" you might ask.

In its simplest form it's merely a collaboration between parties that share the same values.

Sounds easy, right?

Well there's a few pieces to this puzzle to have it run smoothly, but first let's look at the benefits it brings you!

Benefit #1 - Building Your Brand and Fast Tracking Your Reputation

One thing I positively love about partnerships/collaborations, etc. is that you can quickly build both your reputation and your brand in a very short period of time.

Imagine you're just starting out and you collaborate with someone who is a little further down the road from you. They don't have to be that far; just far enough that they have more reach than you do.

Benefit #2 - More Clients and More Revenue in Less Time

Now, as long as you can fulfil all your promises and you have something scalable, you can very quickly have access to more clients that need your service or product.

Benefit #3 - More Partners to Collaborate With

It doesn't take long for someone to see that you are collaborating; believe me us collaborators can smell out a partnership a mile off.

While everyone else is focused on finding one client at a time, your focus will be on one partner at a time; you can easily 10x your business growth this way.

Benefit #4 - Increasing Your Business Multiplier If You Decide To Sell

When you decide to partner, you have to get a lot of systems in place to manage the scale. Having systems in a business increases the value of the business. As does consistent revenue from multiple partners!

"Where did this partner obsession first come from, Pauline?"

I'm glad you asked!

I've been sold on the idea of partnerships ever since I was in a Sales and Business Development position in my late twenties. By the time this is published, I'll be very near to fifty!

Putting it bluntly, I have a tonne of experience in not only forming partnerships, but finding them, connecting with them and nurturing them, getting creative with them and systemising the process—and yes, I'm a tech geek too.

Plus I both receive and give partner referrals on a regular basis.

Most of my working life has involved partnerships. I see partnerships everywhere I look; it's firmly implanted in my psyche.

I've helped companies achieve absolutely epic growth using this strategy. I've researched more websites, offerings and people than I care to mention and I have developed short cuts for just about every element of the partner process.

I still remember the first partnership I ever pulled off. I was desperately trying to fill an event with about 1,500 people and I had a partner who had promised to mail his clients and I wasn't sure exactly when the email was going out.

Then, all of a sudden, the leads started coming in hot and heavy. I've never hit F5 (refresh) so many times in such a short period in my life, boy was I excited!

After an hour, there were 732 registrations!! One email, from one partner, nearly half filled the event, just like that.

I was sold!! "That's it," I thought, "I'm going to master this strategy." And so I did!

Fast forward many years and I've given multiple presentations on the topic, been involved in several entrepreneurial training companies as their partnership mentor and generally continued to help people achieve what I like to call "bums on seats with cash". I guess that will eventually be called "bums on seats with digital currency", but it doesn't quite have the same ring to it!

The thing to keep in mind here is that partners leads are WARM leads; they require no cash to bring them into your business ecosystem.

Generally speaking, they buy much faster and spend more in less time. My husband might say I'm quite capable of doing the same!

Remember, gone are the days of getting Facebook leads for a few cents. All of these advertising companies know they have businesses over a barrel and they will eke out of you whatever they can.

It's not uncommon to be paying from $10 to $50 a lead and that's just to get them to your site; they are cold traffic and require many more touchpoints to buy from you.

So, what do you need for one of these collaborations?

A lot, actually. Which is why I've laid out a bunch of fun tasks that you can load up into your project management software and get cracking!

First and foremost, you need to know how to connect with people. It's rare for someone to collaborate if they don't already have some level of rapport with you.

But don't worry; I'm going to dedicate some time to that shortly.

For now, let's look at what sort of collaboration excites you!

Lucky for you, there's a few different models to choose from.

Task #1 - Identify the types of partnerships that complement your core offering.

These are the key ways you can collaborate and it's important to distinguish between affiliates, partnerships, and joint ventures (JV's).

So, what's the difference?

A partner: Seeks non-monetary returns, such as clients, exposure, or content distribution.

An affiliate: Primarily focuses on earning money through referral commissions.

It's crucial to recognise the difference, as affiliates are often less motivated than partners.

To motivate affiliates, consider offering additional incentives beyond money, like a physical prize for instance. Even a leaderboard can work wonders!

Dealing with multiple affiliates can be time-consuming, so building systems to manage them is necessary - yay, more tech!

You can also choose to reward just your affiliates for their direct referrals, or you can implement a 2 tier structure so you reward them for sales made by people they introduce to the program as well. Whilst I know this sounds a bit like a pyramid scheme, it's not because it stops there.

Joint Ventures: Typically follow collaborative partnerships. Before entering into a legal agreement, consider starting with a collaborative project to gauge compatibility and trust. Dipping a toe in, is a less risky approach.

Once you're happy, consider starting with a more formal arrangement, but don't over complicate it—you merely need a Heads of Agreement.

This is as simple as Party A agrees to do XYZ by time frame and Party B agrees to do ABC by time frame.

From there, it's over to the lawyers to draft something that makes both of you happy.

Task #2 - Brainstorm your perfect product and services partners

Now that you've established the type of partnership that you are looking for, it's time to build a profile of your ideal partner.

Consider the following.

- What compliments your core offering?
- What do people need before they need your products and services?
- What do they need after they've had your products and services?

As you can appreciate, this is different for every business, but it should be quite obvious when you reflect on your customers journey.

When seeking partners, think creatively and maintain an abundance mentality. Unlikely partnerships can often yield the most successful outcomes.

Here are a few unusual partnerships I've encountered over the years:

- A broker and a coffee shop, locality based. The broker offered to pre-pay for 100 coffees and when you entered the cafe, the owner said "hey you want a free coffee? Just fill in this form and your coffee is free." $4 leads in a Million Dollar neighbourhood.
- A financial planner and a beauty salon. The planner was looking for ways to reward their clients for referring, the salon was looking for high net worth clients and offered a mini facial.
- A camera company and a small business event. The small business was looking for credibility and the camera company was looking for exposure into a new market.
- A recent example of a collaboration that has morphed into an acquisition, started as a strategic partnership in the commercial real estate education space. A joint webinar was where it started and eventually, the person who ran the webinar bought the training organisation and the education materials with it.

Task #3 - Find out who offers these products and services in your area

Make a list with the providers of your perfect partner products/services and rate them from top to bottom.

Then actually go to their site and opt in for whatever they have on offer. Put yourself in your client's shoes and think about the value their emails provide and whether you would promote this to your clients.

Shortlist the prospective partners that rate highly, provide lots of value and have a great lead magnet (if you're not sure what a lead magnet is, just read on—I've even put together a mini course on how to create a lead magnet, which you'll find in the resources section at the end of this chapter).

Suggestion! Once you do the whole process yourself, you can outsource the research of the prospects, list creation and shortlist candidates.

Task #4 - Connect with your potential partners

Engage on other social media platforms - Connect on LinkedIn, join Facebook groups - share, like and comment on their posts.

Remember to do this authentically or don't do it at all.

While you're doing that check the comments from their tribe, really think about what you could create in your own lead magnet that would be of massive value.

Because guess what? That's the next step!

Task #5 - This is where the rubber hits the road. You need to set up your lead magnet funnel now.

There is nothing more stressful than building your bike while you're riding it. However, if that's how you're wired, just move on to the next step and come back to this when you have spoken to a receptive partner and had some caffeine!

Otherwise, I highly recommend you engage someone for this step; ideally a tech geek.

I've mentored people that wanted to do this themselves and 6 weeks later they hadn't even decided on a CRM system! Analysis paralysis is a very real phenomena in a space that moves as fast as tech. Pick one and move on or outsource this quick smart.

You'll need a great Lead Magnet / Freebie / Opt-in / Taster, etc.

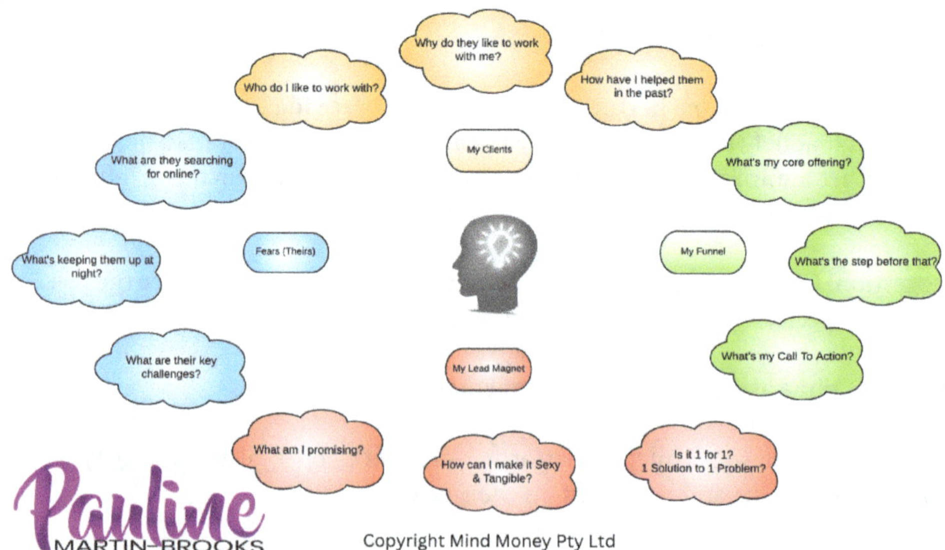

Some examples could be a PDF of the common pitfalls related to your industry that potential buyers ought to be aware of, it could be a mini course on how to achieve something, it could be a free audio download of something that your clients need to know before they work with you. It could be a video presentation with the person you're collaborating with or even a white paper.

There is no end to the creativity you can explore, but stay focused on your client and their burning desires and what's keeping them up at night. Give them something that's hugely valuable that will help them get closer to needing your product or service.

There's a whole training we could do on this, but suffice to say, it's a snippet of how you can help your potential clients. You have to make it enticing enough that someone will leave their name and email in return.

Of course, once your partner has shared your lead magnet and people opt in to your list, you need to nurture them through to the sale.

This process could take days, weeks or months depending on the industry you are in, the value you've provided and the quality of the leads that your partner sends you.

So have a series of small emails which build trust and directs people to blogs you've written.

Haven't written anything yet? How will they know how amazing you are?!

Get some gold out of your head; your expertise needs to be in the world, not just between your ears!

The more you can automate this, the better.

You are essentially dropping someone into your product/service funnel.

So it's ideal to have something in place to re-target the people who don't take action on your lead page.

Make sure you have enough content ready to share when people join your list.

This could be case studies or testimonials of other people overcoming their challenges by using your product or service.

It could be a piece of valuable content that is going to be of benefit to your clients on their buying journey.

Remember to track any touchpoints you have with clients and market to them based on the actions they've taken since getting on your list.

This is why you need a CRM system!

There's nothing more frustrating to me as an automation specialist than getting an email from someone essentially saying 'hey buy my thing', when I've been a loyal client for years!

But Pauline, do I really need all of this? Can't I just offer a free consultation or something?

Well, let's workshop this, shall we? You've decided on your partner type, you've done your research and you've made a call and they've said yes. Woohoo congrats, go you!

Now imagine this consultation takes an hour to fulfil, how scalable is your offer really?

You see the double edged sword with collaborations is leverage.

When things are going well, it can be magnified and help you reach your goals faster.

But what if you can't deliver because you're under-resourced, for instance?

What if instead of giving 10 free consultations, your offer really hit the spot and you got 100 within an hour! What then?

This is where a volume of enquiries that come with these types of collaboration can completely derail your business processes along with the partnership.

To protect and enhance your reputation with partners, please take heed of this advice.

If you can't deliver, i.e. provide great customer experiences for your partners' clients, then don't attempt this strategy until you can.

There's nothing wrong with planting seeds here and there until you're ready but you will ruin your reputation if you can't deliver.

So how do you solve this dilemma?

It's easy if you put together something commonly referred to as a lead magnet funnel.

Oh wait, we just covered that in task #5, remember?!

So can we agree on no consultations as they are not scalable?

Great, let's move on.

Task #6 - What's in it for me?

Now you need to be able to put yourself in your prospective partner's shoes and their clients and answer the following. Because they might just ask you on that first call!

- What are the benefits to you, to them and to both of your clients? Win-win-win.
- Who are you and why should they listen to you?
- What are your values? How do you demonstrate them?
- Who do you help?
- What do you help them with?
- Anything else that stands out about your company versus a competitor?

You're getting closer to making that first call, here's something else you can do to limit the time it takes you to get back to any prospective partners.

Task #7 - Prepare your post-call email template

Re-iterate the benefits of partnering – "I know who you are, I know the value that you bring and I want to share it".

Ask about the next steps – how you can move forward.

Don't sell the sausage, sell the sizzle. Don't put too much into the email. Be respectful of people's time and energy.

Example: Thanks for your time. It was lovely to connect with you. I've been on your list for 3 months and I'm really impressed with what you're sending out. I particularly love your lead magnet. I'd like to talk with you about sharing it with my clients.

Tip: This kicks off the law of reciprocity. The response will be "… what can I do for you?"

Task #8 - Understand how to build strong relationships from the get-go by using Rapport.

Here's a crash course - you can get more information on my resources page at the end of this chapter.

When people genuinely like and trust you, they become more inclined not only to engage in business with you but also to recommend you within their own network.

Therefore, the swifter you can establish rapport with someone, the sooner you can determine if you align and can offer mutual value.

The process of forging rapport is often referred to as "matching" rapport, while the act of disengaging from it is known as breaking rapport. Both of these processes hold immense significance in your partnership journey, so take a deep breath and let's dive in.

The choice of language can be a make-or-break factor. If someone uses a lot of slang, they may not appreciate a conversation in proper English.

It's akin to speaking with someone who's down-to-earth compared to someone who's more refined. Building rapport with them becomes more enjoyable if you adapt your language to match theirs.

When starting a conversation, don't overthink it. One of the most valuable pieces of advice I ever got when I was younger was to be reminded that regardless of who I was calling, they were just another human.

So here's a gentle reminder - whoever you reach out to, just know that they eat, breath and sh*t the same as you.

See now it's easier to call isn't it?!

Once someone starts speaking to you, reference the following to ascertain the best way to truly connect with them:

If they haven't said much, always ask them: "Have I got you at a good time," or "Is now still a good time?"

As long as they say yes then you can continue. Remember, you have 2 ears and 1 mouth - use them in proportion ;)

You can always ask them "how's business at the moment," or "how's your day been," or "how's your morning been," or "have you had a busy day," or "can you believe it's Friday already?" - clearly they are situation-dependent, but you get the gist.

Ask a question and then be quiet and notice which of these types of individuals you are speaking with.

Visual People:

Visual people, like myself, tend to speak rapidly. They also breathe swiftly, primarily using the upper part of their lungs, and they can process ideas and strategies faster than most.

Matching their pace is essential for effective communication. They often use phrases like "Can you see what I'm saying?" or "What does that look like?" When talking to a fast speaker, matching their pace and using these phrases can help build rapport.

Kinaesthetic People:

Are known as "feeling people". They speak, breathe, and process information slowly, making them the opposite of fast speakers.

They are easily recognizable by their slow speech and deep breaths. They often use touch and feeling-related phrases. When speaking with a slow-paced individual, adjust your pace and take deep breaths. Personally if I'm on the phone with one, I close my eyes!

Auditory People:

Have a balanced speaking pace and clear enunciation, resembling a radio announcer. They process information faster than kinaesthetic people but not as fast as visual people. Matching their pace, incorporating pauses, and using auditory related phrases can aid in building rapport.

Auditory Digital People:

Have a logical approach. They speak at an auditory pace and use logic-based phrases and seek a clear understanding of each step. When dealing with them, providing a logical explanation for the process is vital.

Task #9 - Smile and Dial

Refresh yourself with their website / LinkedIn / YouTube channel and look for products or services they offer, about page, team, values and testimonials.

You need to know:

- What the company does
- Who their raving fans are
- The quality of their lead magnet
- Your willingness to share it

Tip: The more you know about each other's businesses, the easier it will be to create a win-win partnership.

Tip: Try to speak to the business owner. Call at about 8.15 am to avoid the "gatekeeper".

Don't like cold calling? That can easily be fixed! Ask me how.

After the call, it's imperative to follow up in a timely manner and deliver on everything you've discussed. Remember that first partnership? The 732 event bookings? Well, that took 6 months!

"The Fortune Is In The Follow Up." - Jim Rohn

Is Partnering For Everyone?

By now you've heard all the reasons as to why now is the right time, all of the benefits of partnering and hopefully you've decided exactly what's in it for you. So… I think it's time to be a little contrarian and discuss why maybe it's not right for you.

Some people I've spoken with legitimately can't collaborate as it's not part of their franchise agreement, so if you're in a franchise, check your agreement first.

You may also be in an industry where you can only collaborate with certain types of businesses and perhaps you can't be seen to favour one over the other. If that's the case, speak with some industry peers to see if there is a way around it before you invest too much time.

Now there's so many different little things that come together to make the perfect partnership and most of them require you to roll up your sleeves and get stuck in.

So if you're not willing to do that, partnerships aren't for you and you should likely stop reading and give this to someone you know who gets stuff done.

If you're a control freak, then this could be a challenging strategy for you for several reasons. Firstly, you need to be able to delegate effectively, i.e. don't be a task hoarder, work out what you can let go and do it! You have to do this to make room for finding partners.

Secondly, partnerships by their very nature depend on other people to do something and let's face it, we are all human and sometimes things happen that are out of your control, so you will have to learn to deal with that.

Why else might you walk away?

Well put frankly, if you're not in it for the long term, walk away now. Partners are precious and you need to remember that. It's a long term strategy and whilst you might not get the perfect win-win the first time around, you've got to have the flexibility to have another go.

And if you're not in it for the win-win, people will see right through you, so don't even bother with this strategy.

Lastly, you need to have flexibility when you're partnering. If you can only think of one way to collaborate and you're not willing to get outside of your box, then maybe this isn't the right strategy for you either.

Key Takeaways For You To Focus On

1. Align with Others Who Share Similar Values
2. Identify Key Benefits to All Parties Involved
3. Leverage Warm Leads Through Partnerships
4. Increase the Overall Value of Your Business
5. Understand How to Effectively Convert Your Leads
6. Have a Flexible Mindset and Focus on the Win-Win

Ready to move forward or just want to know more about this strategy? I'm here to help, so please reach out and let's collaborate!

You can book a 15-minute chat with me on this page or ping me on LinkedIn, I'm fairly certain I'm the only Pauline Martin-Brooks in the world!

Oh and remember…

"The most wasted day of all is that in which we have not laughed!"
- Nicolas Chamfort

For more information about collaborating, systems, email templates and to book me to speak to your audience, please scan the QR code below or go to: *https://paulinemartinbrooks.com.au/resources*

Chapter 8

Unleashing the Power of Belief: A Journey to True Wealth

Jane Slack-Smith

Author, Founder of Investors Choice Mortgages, Your Property Success and Your Success Club

About The Author: Jane Slack-Smith

Jane Slack-Smith is a testament to the power of transformation and tenacity. One of the first females in the New South Wales underground coal mines to a celebrated property investment strategist, Jane has shattered ceilings and built bridges to financial freedom for thousands. A powerful testament to her mantra: anything is possible with will, belief and action.

Her initial success was as an explosives expert in the mining industry. Her pioneering work led her to be featured in ABC's Australian Story and be included in the Who's Who of Australian Women.

Jane transferred her skills in risk assessment to property investing, developing her Trid3nt Strategy®. This led her and her husband to create a large property portfolio. Utilising this personal success, Jane, wanting to share this knowledge, transitioned into finance and investment education, benefiting thousands.

Founding Investors Choice Mortgages in 2005, she claimed business success, winning the Australian Mortgage Broker of the Year award twice. She then co-founded Your Property Success, an online education platform, and authored the book "Your Property Success with Renovation" (Wiley & Sons).

Jane has been featured in several publications, including Money Magazine and The Australian Financial Review. A recognised expert, she has frequently appeared on TV and spoken nationally and internationally. She has been named one of the four most influential figures in personal finance for Australian families. However, what sets Jane apart is her exploration of the science of success and assisting others to achieve it.

Enjoying success in many parts of her life, she is a dedicated student of what stops others from achieving the same. Beyond financial empowerment, Jane is deeply committed to personal growth and philanthropy. Through her company, Your Success Club, she shows how to break through limiting beliefs and live a life of purpose. Now an accredited Natural Success coach, Jane doesn't just teach wealth creation; she mentors on living a life of abundance in all its forms. Jane is a sort-after inspirational speaker at company events. Together with her business coaching clients and money mindset students, she inspires anyone seeking a life filled with purpose, abundance, and impact.

Mine is an unconventional story about my journey to true wealth. It's a tale I'm eager to share because I hope that hearing my story ignites a desire to create your own success.

As I look back on my journey, it is clear to me that the early beliefs we formed in our childhood often go unnoticed, yet they influence our choices throughout our lives. It took me decades to become aware of the underlying stories and the limitations they imposed on me. I had several moments that gave me insights into these patterns playing out, and that allowed me to move forward. Each step transformed me and led me to success. But it didn't come all at once nor quickly. I didn't start with any financial advantages but something a whole lot more valuable: a childhood belief that I was in control of my creations and I could create anything I wanted.

Today, I introduce people to becoming aware of the stories and patterns at play in their lives through an initial exploration of the money stories. I use money as a starting point, as we are all familiar with it. (If you want to learn more about your money stories, I have a special gift for you at the end of this chapter).

I didn't stumble upon success; I pursued it with determination and, more importantly, actions. My journey led me from the male-dominated mining industry as an explosives expert to a multiple award-winning mortgage broker, author, podcaster, and sought-after speaker. I founded successful companies, shared my knowledge, and empowered countless individuals to rewrite their own stories.

This isn't merely my story; it's a testament to the boundless potential within us all. As I share my story, I intend you to uncover the threads that connect my experiences to yours – exposing an awareness of the beliefs that shackle us all and the steps to propel us forward.

Humble Beginnings: A childhood that shaped my beliefs

Growing up in a small farming community in Dubbo, western New South Wales, Australia, wealth was never a topic anyone discussed. In our small town, overseas holidays, lavish homes, and fancy cars were uncommon. My parents worked long hours in physically demanding jobs, as a nurse and a farm manager. Although a modest upbringing, my parents instilled in my sister and me a priceless gift: **belief.** Night after night, they would tuck us in with warm hugs, and my mother would whisper: "You are Jane Slack-Smith. You can do anything but fly, and with God's help, you can even fly." This belief became ingrained in my identity, fostering a profound self-confidence that would later empower me to embrace the world's opportunities, with the certainty that setbacks were not failures but just learning opportunities.

It wasn't until my late 20s, when I gained insight into how not just to identify but expose the functional and, more importantly, usually unconscious and dysfunctional beliefs about myself, money, and how to get success in the world, that I grasped the impact my childhood experiences had forged within me.

A clear memory that sheds light on the roots of my relationship with money is me at age 3, when my parents discovered me feeding $2 notes into the wood-burning stove, bidding farewell to the images of sheep on the Australian currency as they turned to ashes. This memory allowed me to realize why the idea of savings eluded me.

I observed that whenever my parents managed to save, an unforeseen expense would arise, compelling them to dip into their reserves. In my young mind, having money seemed to attract misfortune. This juvenile notion solidified into an unconscious belief that guided my financial decisions.

My father earned extra money growing vegetables to sell in town, and, for a bit of fun, my sister and I often sold surplus vegetables at a stall outside our home. Each sale was promptly followed by a dash to the little corner store to purchase a bag of mixed lollies. I also recall when my mother sent me to the shops to buy milk, I would spend every cent on discounted items, proudly returning home with half-wilted tomatoes and marked-down bread. After all, I saw returning with money still in my pocket as a failure.

My story is not uncommon. When I run courses for my clients, my community and corporations, I take people through an exercise that uncovers the impressions they formed during childhood about money. It quickly shows people how those early experiences have become habits and then patterns that have played out throughout their lives. Without a significant event or one of those 'ahh - ha' moments, it is difficult to see these underlying insidious patterns at play.

One of those awakening moments was when I read the thought-provoking question Robert Kiyosaki asks in his book Rich Dad, Poor Dad, "Do you work for your money, or does your money work for you?" and I was struck by the effect it had on me. It revealed my money story that had been prevalent throughout my life. My pattern was when I got money, I had to spend it. So, despite a very well-paid job and no significant overheads, i.e. family or mortgage, I had no savings. I consoled myself that the holidays and financial support I could provide for my family was worth it. I was living with an old pattern that was keeping me from what I really wanted, which was creating a life of choices. To do what I wanted, when I wanted, with whom I wanted, with no restrictions, financial or otherwise.

When I speak with audiences about their financial mindset, they often realize how their childhood experiences have impacted their relationship with money. And, like me, they previously had no conscious awareness of this pattern continually playing out. My favourite exercise to take people through is my Vision Session, and although I primarily do this as a one-on-one exercise, I also run workshops for large groups. It always surprises me that even in the group environment, the participants have profound experiences.

The Vision Session involves a visualization exercise where you imagine living your ideal life. The approach is meant to create tension between the cost of living your ideal life and the current financial situation you are in. The process involves two frames of reference: where you want to be and where you are now. Once these two positions are clear, the next step is to build a "bridge" between them. For many years, I helped clients create this bridge by investing in residential property. However, now I work with people to create businesses that align with their purpose and help them fill the income gap.

This structured and simple process establishes a relationship between the present and the desired future, resulting in a natural tension between the two points. A fundamental law of nature is that when tension exists, it seeks to be resolved. As an explosives engineer, my job was to make the rock move. I needed to create enough energy that it had to be released from the confines of the drill hole. By putting stemming on top to keep the energy contained, the only way it could resolve the tension was to break the rock on the walls of the drill hole.

There are many examples of this law: the weather, for instance. The air moves from areas of high pressure to areas of low pressure to equalise the pressure. Even in our daily lives, when there is tension with another person, we have a default way to resolve it, either through conflict, negotiation, or cooperation.

This law and structure give us insight. With clarity, we can't hide from our current position; we connect to what is important in our lives, and from this comes the obvious next action to move forward to achieve it. Awareness is the key, and then taking action towards what you want.

An email I received from Don, a chief financial officer, after I presented as part of a company's workforce empowerment program, summed up the whole experience.

He wrote:

"It was such a unique, incredible, and soulful experience for me. We all have our own stories to tell, and we are unique in our own way. Somehow, along the way, I've lost my identity, and at this stage of my life, I have been struggling to figure out what my purpose in life is. What I really want in this life. I am so grateful that the company invested in you. I would not have done this myself, but I realize now it was priceless.

When we looked into what we wanted to create in our lives, I was expecting something like to be a millionaire or billionaire. Riches of this Earth. A million-dollar house. A luxury car. But it's not. That's not me. You showed me what was important, and with that comes great relief. I know going forward, I choose the end result of … believing in my own greatness, and living a life of gratitude."

Imagine, as an employer, giving your employees a reason 'why' and a newfound commitment and focus to their role. That is a far cry from some of my workplace experiences.

Where there is will - there is a way

I had many more opportunities to consider my beliefs and expose those not working in my favour.

At the end of my schooling, the path to success appeared clear: university was the gateway to financial stability. It promised a way to a comfortable life where lack of money would not restrict me and would enable me to support my parents, who had sacrificed so much for my sister and me.

Yet, there was a glaring obstacle: we needed a way to fund my university education. So, with my parents, we embarked on a mission to help me secure a scholarship. I remember vividly the hours spent in our lounge, meticulously addressing envelopes to top Australian companies, each containing an enquiry for information about scholarships. The prospect of a university degree held immense promise; I aspired to delve into public relations, media, or marketing, although fate had different plans.

Despite doing well in interviews and achieving good grades, the scholarships offered were not in my desired field. Then came a twist of fate - I was awarded a scholarship to study Mining Engineering.

Nonetheless, I embraced the opportunity and embarked on my university journey. The School of Mines was more accustomed to seeing male students, and five young women in a class of thirty was a notable anomaly. Gender biases were prevalent from the first day when an older professor, unapologetically chauvinistic, relegated us to the back row, believing our sole purpose was to find a husband.

Throughout my fifteen-year tenure in the mining industry, I encountered numerous individuals with antiquated mindsets. Moreover, I didn't anticipate that my mere presence would catalyse a strike involving over three hundred men. In December 1989, I ventured into my first underground coal mine, unaware that earlier that year, New South Wales had finally revoked laws prohibiting women from working in such mines. Unbeknownst to me, I was a test subject for this groundbreaking change.

My arrival prompted immediate resistance from mine union officials who believed it was bad luck to have a woman underground, fearing that my presence could bring disaster. Their solution was to dress me in white paper overalls so the men could see me coming! A small oversight was that in the very wet underground environment, paper dissolves, something they overlooked in favour of protecting my female sensitivity. Despite an awkward beginning, I forged strong bonds with my crew.

Transitioning to an open-cut coal mine as a young engineer brought new challenges. I adopted an unconventional approach to preparing for the 7 a.m. daily mine operation meeting. I would turn up at 5 a.m. to spend time with the maintenance crew and drive around the pit with the night shift manager to grasp the nuances of what had contributed to the results of the previous 24 hours. I learnt that getting insights at the "coalface" gave me a better understanding.

Jane at the coal face

When it was time for a new job, I contacted friends in the mining industry and asked if they worked with someone inspiring. Finally, a friend came back with a name. So I researched him and the company he worked for and found that not only did the company offer fantastic world-class training, they had a current job opening for an explosives engineer. Why not? That sounded like fun.

So, I uplifted my life and moved to a new state to start a career as an explosives expert. I had completed my thesis at university on a new technique - Risk Assessments - and this was a perfect opportunity to implement this expertise. A focus on safety would be more critical in the future; the problem was it often took years for others to see the dots I had already connected.

The same happened years later when I was awarded a prestigious Winston Churchill Fellowship to study "Innovative techniques, using explosives, for mine site rehabilitation". On my return from those months of world travel, I compiled innovative practices to rehabilitate mines, and I was excited to share them. However, it proved too innovative, and it wasn't until 22 years later that a company reached out to learn more about my groundbreaking environmental technique.

Throughout my life experiences, I have always been driven by my desire to create. I have always held the belief that I am capable of achieving anything I set my mind to, and I have never been afraid to take the necessary steps to make my dreams a reality. My unique ability to connect people, ideas, and concepts and see a bigger picture or a future trend has been core to my success. However, the most important factor has been to take action, an area where many people often fall short.

The Entrepreneurial Leap: Building Wealth and Independence

Homeownership was never something I wanted. I didn't want the white picket fence that became a financial prison. However, my husband and his can-do attitude by my side showed me that your first property didn't have to be a home. Together, property investing became a passionate pursuit for us.

This path led us to financial security and the ability to pursue new careers not limited by financial constraints. I had gained my goal - freedom of choice. With each property, I honed my strategies and deepened my understanding of the market and what the renters and subsequent buyers wanted. I also researched to minimise my risk and put together several indicators that allowed us to purchase in areas that were going up in value and were in demand and hence develop a unique and highly profitable strategy – The Trid3nt Strategy ®. I shared this with my friends and family, and they also created portfolios to give them financial security and a path to achieving their own freedom goals.

By harnessing my strengths in minimising risk gleaned from my university thesis and daily practice as an explosives engineer and my unique ability to suspend the conventional path and connect the dots of apparently unrelated information to the property buying process, I amplified my investments and accelerated my wealth-building journey. The world of finance, once daunting and mystifying, began to make sense.

This innovative approach appealed to my desire for flexibility and financial growth. It was a revelation that reshaped my thinking and prompted me to embark on a mission: to share this knowledge with others who were also seeking financial freedom so they could pursue their true passions and purpose.

I jumped from a corporate role with a stable income and career opportunities into a commission-based business with no clients but with an unwavering belief that I could transform lives. I boldly embraced my newfound purpose. However, I didn't just wish it would happen and expect clients and a successful business to evolve. I took action. I made a blueprint for best practices (by cheekily contacting the top 30 mortgage brokers in the business with a list of questions) before I even opened my doors - combining this with research of my ideal client's pains, fears, and desires, I minimised the business risk. With the skills and success I had, I was able to create a niche and a detailed ideal client analysis. I used that to find a perfect collaboration partner and a speaking platform to find those clients and create for them a detailed journey focussed on their success.

This business startup plan differs from the typical path of a mortgage broker who was a banker previously and used their friends, families, and real estate agents to get business. Despite not having experience, I started on a path that I would continue for the next 20 years. And it always began with a coach who had succeeded in the field. I combined their learnings with my unique approach to leapfrog over challenges. For my clients, I was not just thinking of their current property purchase but rather why they were doing it all in the first place, their ideal life, and their end goal. This unique method paid off; I was awarded, not once but twice, Australian Mortgage Broker of the Year.

I started sharing my knowledge on stages and anywhere I could. I graced the cover of property magazines and Money Magazine, which resulted in me being named one of the four most significant financial influencers in Australia.

In 2012, one of my students and I co-founded a business to educate people on these strategic property investing techniques. I was at the helm of a thriving community, all driven by the desire to secure their financial future through property.

Reflecting on my journey from the small farming community of Dubbo to the bustling world of property investing, I am reminded of the power of holding the vision of what you want to create. It was the unwavering belief instilled in me by my parents that fueled my confidence and the will to take bold action. The ability to hold focus on my end goal, my vision, was apparent through all my undertakings.

I have exercised this unapologetic notion of going successfully for my end goal and calling on my 'resilience resume' built up through my many experiences. One that comes to mind includes being diagnosed with Cushing's disease. I had a brain tumor on my pituitary gland. From the diagnosis through to recovery, I had the belief I could create an ideal surgical experience with a fast and complete recovery, which I did. Even the surgeon was shocked the 4-hour scheduled surgery took 2 hours. We still laugh today over who was responsible for that outcome. The focus exercises of my desired result that I did leading to the surgery, was exactly how he explained it occurred.

Incidentally, whilst in recovery 30 minutes after the completion of brain surgery, I was running my first of many masterclasses for the nurses on the dynamics that would affect the wealth they could accumulate in their first home purchase. After all, I never miss an opportunity to share my knowledge.

In 2021, I undertook the five-day Cradle Mountain Overland (mainly up mountains) trek in Tasmania. It was not until I was introduced to the ten-person cohort that I realised not only had they climbed the most famous peaks in the world and were seasoned on gruelling climbs as preparation for the trek, but that I, who had not even worn a backpack, let alone worn in my walking shoes, was going to have to draw on the past experiences from my resilience resume and put my focus on successfully completing that trek to get me through. And I did. Focusing on my end result, with the certainty of its successful achievement, is now just part of who I am.

Awareness is the key. Being aware of the stories and patterns at play, mainly from our underlying beliefs, and then consciously focusing on what you really want to create can turn that into reality.

But what I realised, having taught tens of thousands of would-be wealth creators through my property investing courses and workshops, was that some were creating wealth and others were not.

This perplexed me. The fact that some people, despite having everything at their fingertips, still didn't make a sound decision—or even worse, no decision—astounded me. So, I got to work on finding out why.

What I found shocked me. Digging deeper, I found that those who were fearful of taking action in investing also showed the same inaction in their relationships, careers, and health. I realised that how you do anything is how you do everything. But what was driving this behaviour?

I realised that the end goal most concentrated on was escaping or moving from what they DIDN'T want rather than what they desired. In other words, they had a negative vision, i.e. not wanting to be lonely, poor, or overweight, and that is what they were creating.

I had spent 20 years teaching people how to buy property, but I was missing the point. I, like them, assumed that they first had to have a successful property portfolio before they could have the life they desired.

Then I heard this quote from Bishop Desmond Tutu:

"I was spending all my time pulling drowning people from the river, but I realised if I went upstream, I could prevent them jumping in."

I realised that's what I was doing for some in my community. Even though I gave them education and guidance, with my (misguided) belief that this wealth would provide them with the freedom to pursue their dreams, I realised no matter how much help and resources I gave them, some were not taking action, some did the opposite to what I was teaching, and some oscillated between action and inaction, with no consistent results.

So I 'went upstream' and today, through my workshops, podcast, speaking events and online community, I help people learn how to uncover their underlying beliefs, create that positive vision of the life they truly want, take action, and achieve true wealth and abundance in all aspects of their lives.

It has taken me decades to become aware of the functional and dysfunctional beliefs and how they have driven my choices professionally and personally. Today, it still takes will to stay alert to those familiar patterns.

Although I have created financial wealth, it is the true wealth that I have created for my life that I am most proud of and that I am excited to share. The easiest path to seeing the stories that shape us is through the money stories we have, and so, as a first step, that is how I introduce people to an awareness of what is driving their actions, not just in their financial decisions but in all aspects of their lives. These patterns are playing out in all areas of our lives - relationships, careers, health - and informing our decisions.

I have been a curious adventurer with a clear focus on my goals, and I believe I am the master of creating them. Despite this focus leading me into some unconventional careers and ways I operate my companies, I have created true wealth and love helping others do the same.

I challenge people to ask themselves: Which patterns are unconsciously holding you from creating true and meaningful abundance in your life?

For more information about the courses, coaching and speaking opportunities with me, please scan the QR code below or go to www.yoursuccessclub.com.au

And as promised, to learn more about your personal Money Stories, you can complete this short quiz *https://yoursuccessclub.com.au/s/money-mojo* to give you insights, and if you join my Facebook group *https://www.facebook.com/groups/yoursuccessclubtoday* I'd love to gift you with the first module of my course 'Renovate Yourself Renovate Your Wealth' so you can take the first step to create abundance in all aspects of your life.

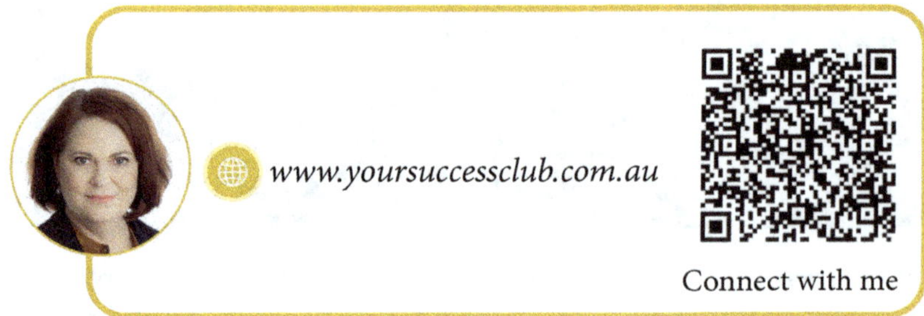

Chapter 9

Influencing Your Event Audience with Presentation, Staging and Video

Martin Renaud
Founder of Freedom Potential Pty Ltd

About The Author: Martin Renaud

20 years ago, I was experimenting with technologies in multimedia theatre that has now become the standard in events and conferences: multi-camera live streaming, video projection mapping and blending, audio line arrays… I was producing shows with my company P: Media Arts and innovating by integrating electronic devices in all types of productions.

Based in Quebec City, Canada, I started touring my projects across the country, in Australia and internationally. I produced a multimedia experimental dance show in Melbourne for Commonwealth Games 2006 before settling in 2008, where I became Executive Director of Open Channel, a Film and TV school in the Docklands. My organisation was producing 4 events per week, with various stakeholders and delivering RTO courses to 1500 students per year. Open Channel was then producing 50+ short films and documentaries per year.

This is where I got my first hands-on experience in planning and producing events, as well as with all the technical aspects of such endeavours, all the more eclectic: drive-in cinemas, outdoor concerts, conferences, screenings and other large scale entertainment for up to 5000pax. In 2010, I moved to Sydney and managed Metro Screen Hire and Facilities department, where I started live-streaming events and managing an equipment hire company.

This brings us to 2015, where I launched my first video production business which I rolled over into Freedom Potential Pty Ltd. Since 2019, I have live-streamed more than 500 events and worked with 250+ clients: speakers, educators, innovators and SMEs looking at creating content economically with high production value. We have catered for the start-up/innovation community, fintech, charities, NGOs and many corporate clients before and during the pandemic with our hybrid studio on the Gold Coast.

The years 2022-2023 have brought me to consult and contract on the largest events in Sydney and in Australia in my speciality (Vision) at ICC Sydney (International Convention Centre) and 40+ hotels venues with Encore Events and Technologies, as a Senior Technician. As a Producer and Technical Director with 20+ years experience, I am constantly pushing the bar for excellence in events production.

Hosting a successful event is a complex art; one that involves orchestrating multiple elements that culminate in a captivating experience for your audience. Whether you're planning a corporate conference, a live performance, or any other event, one of the most critical components of your presentation is driven by audio-visual elements (Audio - Ax, Vision - Vx, Lighting – Lx and Staging/ Rigging). These technical aspects play a pivotal role in captivating your audience, keeping them engaged, and leaving a lasting impression.

The following chapter is an unusual foray into the world of event AV, the industry standard workflows and my experience as the Head of Production of Freedom Potential, with an array of speakers, educators, entrepreneurs and visionaries as clients. A 20-year journey that took me from multimedia experimental dance and theatre, producing shows for the Commonwealth Games 2006 and ISEA 2013, Internationally in Canada, Australia, USA, Indonesia, etc., and having contracted on some of the largest events in Australia in recent years (FIFA Women's World Cup, SXSW Sydney, Sydney World Pride).

In the next few pages, we will delve into the various strategies and technologies involved in creating a mesmerizing event, from technical stage elements to portable AV kits and video production.

Staging AV

The stage is the central platform where your event comes to life. An impressive stage design and well-managed backstage logistics will contribute greatly to the success of your event. From sound design to lighting and video elements, the technical aspects of the stage are fundamental to the impactful delivery of your message. Whether you are selling from the stage or have a more educational approach, a poor staging AV will cost you dearly and a well-crafted technical will increase your yield and authority.

Sound Design

Sound is an integral part of any live event. It is probably the most crucial as proper sound design ensures your audience can hear every word, every note, and every sound effect as intended. There are many aspects that will contribute to your audio delivery that must be addressed during pre-production to ensure the most reliable sound fidelity during your event.

On that note, don't be the speaker that books a hotel venue with the included ceiling speakers with a lapel + a handheld microphone and a "roaming" technician… You are exposing yourself and your audience to horrible audio feedback and no one to turn it off when someone steps under a speaker with a microphone in hand! Cue unstoppable screeching sounds and half your audience leaving the room. Yes, this has happened before…

Rule #1 – Always have a dedicated sound engineer for any and every event! Have another one – a monitor engineer – side of stage, if you are hiring a music band.

Rule #2 – Avoid meeting rooms ceiling speakers, their purpose is to play background music; they are not designed for live events. Hire a PA or on a large stage, a set of speakers in a line array and subwoofers tuned to the venue for clear and even sound across your audience.

Microphones

Selecting the right microphones is crucial for clear and crisp audio. Depending on your event's size and nature, you may need a variety of microphones, including dynamic and condenser microphones with various pickup patterns in different form factors: headset, lavalier and handheld microphones.

Dynamic/Condenser Microphones

Dynamic microphones are great for live performances, as they are less sensitive to feedback and handle high sound pressure levels well. These are typically your gooseneck lectern and lavaliere (lapels) microphones.

Condenser microphones are more sensitive and capture a wider frequency range, making them suitable for spoken word or recording instruments. These are typically used in proximity to the sound source, such as with a headset or acoustic guitar/ drum / wind or brass musical instruments.

Headset Microphones

Headset microphones such as DPA or Countryman are the staple of the industry for stage presenters. It allows for consistent voice pick-up due to the capsule (the tip of the microphone) remaining at the same distance from the mouth when fitted properly over ears and across the back of the head. Some speakers like to own their own professional quality headset (over $1000), but any respectable production company would supply those on hire. Headsets are preferable to lavaliere (lapel) microphones as they allow the speaker to roam on stage hand-free and modulate the best voice audio pattern.

Tip #1 – Avoid dangling earrings or any jewellery that can interfere with the microphone.

Tip #2 – Place the microphone on the cheek or on the side of the lip and test to avoid breathing noises.

Lectern Gooseneck Microphones

Gooseneck microphones are often seen on lecterns on stage, sometimes on one side or on both side of the lectern for best pick-up and redundancy. These are dynamic microphones and will pick up surrounding sounds, such as manipulating notes and tapping on the lectern. If badly equalised by the sound engineer, you could even hear thumping while walking up to the lectern on stage…

To use a gooseneck lectern microphone properly:

1. Stand behind the lectern within a metre of the microphone
2. Keep speaking in the direction of the microphone
3. Do not tap, adjust or touch the microphone unless it hides your face
4. Avoid more than one person at a time behind the lectern.

A typical adjustment to a lectern gooseneck microphone is to create an equaliser envelope with low sensibility in the bass frequencies, a dip in the mid-frequencies (400-500KhZ) and a decent amount of audio compression to allow for an even sound pick up even when the speaker is moving back and forth from the lectern.

Lavaliere (lapel) Microphones

Lavaliere microphones are also used as a hand-free alternative that allow for freedom of movement. They are best used for sit-down interviews and panels when speakers remain in the same position for a long period of time but would not roam on stage or off stage. Lavaliere can also be used to mic up quickly a wind instrument such as a didgeridoo for a Welcome to Country introduction or an organ in a Church.

Lavaliere are typically worn on the button hole side of shirts and coats (on the left side for men and right side for women clothing). Their wire must be hidden, either by threading them through a shirt or by looping back into a coat inside pocket. The belt pack of a wireless lavaliere can be clipped on your belt, bra or neck of a shirt/blouse. For best practice, your sound engineer will power lock your lavaliere transmitter so it can be operated from the sound desk, or you may insist on controling your transmitter for muting at will.

Tip #3 – Avoid cheap wireless audio devices at all costs. It doesn't matter if they are cheap or really cheap. They will pick-up interference and sound crappy. Remember: ALWAYS hire a sound engineer!

Handheld Microphones

These are the microphones you would expect a singer to use and the most common type of microphone. They're also the most versatile. Make sure to always have a couple of extra "handhelds" available as a backup!

The most common microphone of this type is the Shure SM57, which is robust and always sounds great, so long as it is used correctly...

Tip #4 – keep the capsule of the handheld condenser microphone on your chin and speak directly into it. Let the sound engineer adjust the volume for your voice!

AVOID: taking the microphone lower or away from your mouth. Do not tap on it to check if it works, simply catch the attention of the sound engineer to know the line is open.

Specialised Microphones

There are many other specialised microphones that can play a great role in your sound design and that are best left to your sound engineer to recommend. Here are a few types you can use for a production with more nuances:

1. Boom microphone – can be used to pick up a special item on stage (i.e. spinning wheel of fortune, motor engine, craft activity or scribbling, etc) or to record the audience reaction.

2. Instruments microphones – most musical instruments have a dedicated microphone with clips or attachments and are tuned for optimal sound.

3. Intercom – an intercom can be used for "Voice of God" announcements.

Sound Systems

Choosing an appropriate sound system is essential. The size of your venue and the number of attendees will determine the power and coverage required. A sound system consists of amplifiers, speakers, signal processors and sound mixers. It's essential to have a balance between power and clarity to ensure everyone in the audience can hear with precision. This will be determined by the type of content you will be delivering (presentations, video playback, live music, DJ, etc).

Nowadays, most Powered Amplified speakers (PA) will deliver acceptable sound across all content, but medium to large venues will benefit from a suspended line array of speakers and subwoofer on the ground to control the sound more directionally. While a signal processor is necessary, it is usually embedded in analog and digital mixers. The latter are preferred for their ability to monitor the fundamental frequencies of the venue to "ring" the room, meaning finding the problematic frequencies that will create feedback at higher volume. Digital mixing desks also have a better system to route audio in and out devices, recording and more precise equalising for adjusting the voice sound.

Tip #4 – Use a digital desk with automixing or "Dan Dugan" algorithm when holding panels and multiple microphones on stage at the same time, such as Yamaha TF and QL series or DigiCo.

Stingers and Music

Stingers, or sound effects, can add drama and impact to your event. Typically, stingers are either a short and punchy music track or a portion of a song played when a new speaker walks on stage. A commanding walk-on stinger at the beginning of the event and repeated throughout is a powerful emotional anchor for your audience, especially in a sales event or to build influence.

Remember to clear the copyrights for the music you play during your event, as it will become embedded in your livestream and recordings. Alternatively, you can use music composed specifically for your event or royalty-free music. Multiple websites nowadays offer free or cheap alternatives to music covered under standard copyright, such as AI-generated or Creative Commons music.

Additionally, carefully curated background music can set the mood and enhance the overall experience.

Tip #5 – Provide a dedicated phone, tablet or PC to your sound engineer with playback software such as Qlab or a subscription to YouTube, Spotify, Soundcloud for your BGM (background music).

Light Design

Lighting is an often-underestimated aspect of stage design, yet it plays a vital role in setting the ambiance, creating focus, and guiding the audience's attention. Unfortunately, a lack of attention to lighting doesn't only affect the live audience perception but it can literally ruin your video recordings as most cameras will struggle to capturie the subject and environment in low light. At a minimum, you should seek a stage wash and/or spotlight for your speaking position on stage.

And you might be asking: why would I want to wash the stage? Isn't that the janitors job?

Stage Wash

A stage wash is a basic lighting technique that provides even, general lighting across the entire stage. It ensures that all performers are visible and that the stage doesn't look flat. It is usually provided from a Front of House (FOH)—meaning in front of the stage—or back of the room position, either on flown trusses in the roof or on heavy duty stands.

Uplights

Uplighting fixtures are used to highlight elements on the stage, such as set pieces or performers. They can create depth and dimension to the stage. Nowadays, you can purchase cheap LED lights that are battery operated and can be set to your brand's colours. In addition to positioning them on stage, they are often used around the venue and in the foyer to create an atmosphere.

Movers

Moving lights, or "movers," are fixtures that can pan, tilt, and change colors. They add dynamic effects and can be used to create excitement, dramatic shifts, and special moments during an event. Using movers to create "chases", which are a string of bulbs that light up in order to create a moving effect on walls, stage and venue. This is great for arrival and during breaks.

Movers are also used for "Ballyhoo", a swiping lighting state used for welcoming someone one stage, especially used for awards ceremonies or for any winner. This is a great way to make someone feel special while walking up on stage.

"Pin lighting" is another important state of lighting for an event as its typically used to light every table or individual objects in a venue. For a dinner gala or a mastermind type of event with round tables it creates an intimate atmosphere for each group in the room as opposed to turning on the harsh "house lights"

Video Design

Video elements are a powerful tool for engaging and connecting with your audience. They support the content directly with graphics, clips and camera feeds. Video design encompasses the use of projectors, LED screens, fold-back monitors, and teleprompters. Each of those video outputs in the venue require a source for playback and a processor/video switcher for the correct routing of the video elements and create an orchestrated visual impact for the audience.

Projectors

Projectors are used to display visuals, presentations, videos, and "Image Magnification" – IMAG. Most venues are fitted out with projectors that should be appropriate for the size and typical use case of the room. Be mindful that lighting sources will compete with projectors and might need a boost, either with a projector with a brighter output or with "stacking"; effectively adding the brightness of multiple superimposed projectors.

Projectors are usually rigged in the ceiling to avoid their light beam being obstructed. If you install your projector from the ground, you will have to clear the space in front of it to avoid casting a shadow by walking or standing in front of it. Another option to avoid casting a shadow while walking on stage is to use rear-projection by installing a screen that allows for the projector to be placed behind the screen, back of stage. While the brightness output will be dimmer, it allows for more flexibility for the show on stage.

Some advanced uses of projectors, especially in large venues, are projector blends and mapping, which are technical terms for adding multiple projectors to create wide or extra wide custom size content or highlight architectural features of the venue. This is a modern way to impress your audience with displaying your event content and creates a powerful statement that you mean business!

This is all well and good, but you might ask, what should be displayed on projector screens? First and foremost, projectors and LED screens (see below) are used to show event graphics and presentation. Most presentations are played from PowerPoint or Keynote (Mac), Google Slide or similar software. Other, more professional software such as Millumin, ProPresenter, and Resolume allow for building presentations with multiple layers and playback features.

In a medium to large venue, it is usually necessary to magnify the presenter on stage with a camera close-up projected on screens, usually on each side of the stage. This is called IMAG, standing for Image Magnification.

Tip #6 – When preparing your presentation or slide deck, always download all your assets (videos, fonts, images and audio tracks) and deliver them to your AV operator. Avoid using links within your presentation and don't present from a cloud service such as Canva or Google Slides.

Tip #7 – Always prepare a holding slide for your event that can be taken to the screen at any time from setup to pack-down, during breaks and as a backup in case of technical difficulties.

LED Screens

LED screens are highly versatile and offer vivid high-resolution visuals. Nowadays, large events and digital marketing displays are using LED technology for high brightness and custom sized/shaped presentations. Coupled with a signal processor and a production switcher, LED allows us to design multi-layered effects with Picture in Picture effects or graphic overlays that enhance any event.

These LED screens, even in the smaller sizes, are still very expensive to hire, as they are fragile and require highly specialised technicians and many hours to setup. An important thing to consider when hiring LED screens for your event is to design your presentation for the size/aspect ratio of the screen and adjust the brightness if used with other projectors to avoid discrepancy between the intensity of each of your stage displays.

Fold Back Monitors

Fold back monitors, also known as stage monitors, are essential for providing performers with a clear view of the content being displayed. In conferences and speaker events, there could be multiple fold back monitors or DSM (Down Stream Monitors) usually placed directly on stage or at the bottom of stage and inclined for best viewing angle from the speaker.

Fold back monitors might display the current slide of a speaker presentation or the "presenter mode" with the current and next slide. It can also be used as a confidence monitor, showing the camera on screen or livestreaming to allow the presenter to know how to position themselves on stage. They can also have a timer, useful to stay on schedule and show questions or comments from apps such as Slido or real-time sales figures.

Teleprompter

Teleprompters are another type of fold back monitors which are used for live presentations, speeches, or scripted content. They display the script to the presenter, helping them maintain eye contact with the audience while delivering a seamless and confident performance.

Teleprompters can be triggered by speech and other mechanical devices but in events are usually operated by a dedicated technician who will follow your speech and roll the script for you.

Portable Studio / AV Kits

In today's world, flexibility and mobility are key. Speakers, coaches, educators and entrepreneurs often need to deliver presentations while on the road or virtually to events across the world. Portable AV kits enable you to take your event on the road, ensuring you can deliver a top-notch presentation, even in unconventional settings. This is a specialised service of Freedom Potential, where we design, set up and offer training for purpose-made portable studios and AV kits.

Choosing the Right Camera

Selecting the right camera for your portable AV kit is crucial. You'll need a camera that offers the right balance between portability and functionality but with the required features for the type of content and events you will be using it for. Options range from compact DSLRs to camcorders and even high-end smartphone cameras. There are many different types of cameras and it is sometimes the most costly piece of equipment for a portable production kit, and yet it can be its biggest pitfall.

It is usually better to leave this aspect to professionals, however, here are a few aspects to consider:

1. **Powering up the camera** – video camera for events must be powered by constant electric current and therefore you should avoid using batteries because they need to be changed during the event. USB webcams are usually

powered by the computer they are attached to. Mirrorless, camcorders or cinema cameras use an A/C adapter to connected to an electric outlet. PTZ cameras, similar to CCTV can be powered by POE (Power Over Ethernet) cables.

2. **Who will operate the camera?** – Will you set up a still shot with the camera and stand in front of it? A good quality USB webcam, high-end phone or mirrorless could be a good choice. Will you hire an operator to move the camera, on a tripod, gimbal or other type of mounting? In that case, a manual/automatic camera such as a mirrorless, cinema or broadcast camera is a better option for the best quality imaging. Could it be operated remotely or automatically? Consider a PTZ (Pan, Tilt and Zoom) camera can be operated via a joystick or pre-recorded positions or a conference style USB camera with AI tracking capability.
3. **How is the camera being monitored and recorded?** – Another main consideration for acquiring a camera is how it will be monitored and how it will record, in which format? USB web cameras usually don't have recording functionality and the monitoring is done in software. You will need to record with your web conferencing platform or with third party software such as OBS or a proprietary app which will be stored on your computer hard drive. Similarly, a PTZ camera will be recorded on a hard drive attached to a computer or server, however most will have monitoring outputs in HDMI or SDI formats to attach a screen directly to them. Mirrorless, cinema and broadcast cameras uses different types of storage such as SSD, SD, CFast, P2 cards, etc. They will require a card reader and possibly a redundant solution such as an external monitor/recorder. They will typically have one or multiple outputs for monitoring.

Mixing Video and Audio on the Go

When creating a portable AV kit, it's important to have the ability to mix video and audio on-site. This includes using mixers for both video and audio signals, ensuring the final output is of the highest quality. Some brands such as Roland, Rode and Blackmagic have lines of AV mixers that can mix professional video and audio in one package. One advantage of mixing/switching audio and video sources while recording is to cut at the time of editing and post-production by recording the outgoing program immediately. A couple of excellent options are the Blackmagic Design Video Assist and the Atomos line of monitors/recorders.

Microphones

Portable AV kits should include a variety of microphones to suit different situations (see Microphones) as well as an audio signal processor, either included in the video switcher system as per Uplights or as sound mixing console with high quality pre-amps. As a rule of thumb, provision for at least 2 wireless microphones with headsets and/or lavalier for presenters, as well as 2 handhelds for Q&A and panels. Shure, Sennheiser and Sony are favorite brands for professional equipment while Rode and DJI have decent prosumer solutions. Avoid any cheap gear for audio design, as sound for events and recordings is unredeemable…

Road Cases and Suitcases

Proper storage and transportation are essential for your portable AV kit. Road cases and suitcases designed for AV equipment protect your gear while ensuring ease of transport and setup. Many types of cases for AV equipment and especially designed for DJs and audio engineering have a perfect ratio of space counted in "Rack Units" (RU) that helps you to decide how to fit all the equipment within a single box. Many accessories, such as drawers and laser cut made-to-measure foam fillings, patch bay and RU rows of individualised connectors allow to customise each case for your exact needs.

Suitcases and especially Pelican cases are also a good DIY option that allow you to organise a portable kit and travel easily, either with handle or on wheels.

Internet Connection Management

In the digital age, having a reliable internet connection is crucial for live streaming, video conferencing, and other online aspects of your event. Effective internet connection management includes backup solutions to prevent disruptions. At a minimum, any livestream kit should have a redundancy internet system.

It's usually acceptable to use the internet connection in a venue, however the connection and bandwidth allocated should be reserved for the livestreaming only and not for all guests at the event. This would expose the livestreaming feed to failure. A redundancy internet source such as a portable 4G/5G device is recommended, as well as a small router with load balancing or internet bonding capability. Load balancing is when the internet bandwidth load is shared between two or more sources, while internet bonding combines the bandwidth of multiple sources to increase its capacity. Those methods both improve the stability of a livestreaming feed.

Professional bonding equipment includes products from Teradek, PepLink and VidiU. However, many recent routers (such as Netgear and my favorite, GliNet) will support load balancing.

Livestreaming Devices

Including livestreaming devices in your portable AV kit allows you to broadcast your event to a global audience. This is especially important for reaching remote or virtual attendees and extending your event's reach. Most webcams or conference cameras will connect directly to a PC with USB and will use the webconference or live streaming software (such as Zoom and Teams) to capture the video and image signal from cameras. The UVC standard connects external cameras through a USB encoder; it allows you to plug in a mirrorless or broadcast camera to a signal processor and use these cameras for livestreaming and monitoring.

There are also video encoders with livestreaming capability that will encode your videos and audio and push the signal directly to a streaming service such as Youtube or Facebook, Vimeo, Streamyard, etc.

Video Production

Video production is a multi-faceted discipline that encompasses everything from recording and editing to livestreaming and creating compelling highlight reels.

Highlight Reels

Highlight reels are condensed video compilations of your event's most memorable moments. They serve as a powerful marketing tool, showcasing the event's success and creating excitement for future ones.

IMAG (Image Magnification)

Image Magnification, or IMAG, is the process of projecting live footage of performers or speakers onto large screens. This ensures that even audience members seated far from the stage have a close-up view of the action.

Livestreaming

Livestreaming is a game-changer in the event industry. It allows you to reach a global audience in real time, enabling virtual attendees to participate in your event. Livestreaming can be achieved through various platforms, including social media and dedicated streaming services.

Hybrid Events

Hybrid events combine in-person and virtual components, allowing attendees to choose how they want to participate. This approach increases the event's accessibility, extends its reach, and accommodates those who may not be able to attend in person.

Conclusion

In the ever-evolving landscape of event planning and execution, the impact of presentation, staging and video cannot be overstated. These technical strategies are the pillars that support your event's success, captivating your audience and leaving a lasting impression.

From sound design that ensures every word is heard to lighting that creates the perfect atmosphere, and video elements that engage both in-person and virtual attendees, each aspect contributes to the overall experience. Portable AV kits provide the flexibility to take your show on the road, ensuring you can deliver a high-quality presentation wherever your audience may be.

Video production, including highlight reels, IMAG, live streaming, and hybrid events, opens new avenues for engagement, reaching a broader and more diverse audience. As technology continues to advance, event planners and organizers have an array of tools and strategies at their disposal to create unforgettable experiences.

In the end, the success of your event hinges on your ability to master these technical aspects, combining them seamlessly to create a symphony of sound, light, and visuals that will leave your audience inspired and wanting more.

Chapter 10

Presence: The #1 Solution to Your Leadership Challenges

Timothy Carroll
#1 Best-selling Author, Entrepreneur, Public Speaker

About The Author: Timothy Carroll

Timothy Carroll is a New Zealand international, Amazon #1 best-selling author, entrepreneur, champion in barefoot water-skiing and public speaker.

Timothy builds present, purpose driven, high performing leaders. After going through a mid-life crisis in his early 20's, Timothy moved to Sydney, Australia where he trained and worked with the world's best leadership trainers. Leaders such as Tony Robbins, Stephen Covey, and Brian Tracey. Timothy is a pioneer performance coach; over the last 25 years, he has coached world class athletes and business leaders to exceed their potential and goals.

Timothy has worked with Fortune 500 companies, elite sporting organisations, and family businesses on 3 different continents around the world. Some of his many clients include Schneider Electric, The Swedish Golf Federation and The Bahamas Olympic Committee. Timothy is in demand as a speaker delivering key notes on physical and virtual stages alike. He runs his own virtual live events, supporting leaders to be super present, and get back in control of their life.

In 2008, he attended the famous World Equestrian Festival, CHIO Aachen, and later that year the Beijing Olympics as a performance coach for a Swedish Eventing rider. Sweden placed 2nd and 4th overall respectively. An avid sportsman from childhood, Timothy competed for New Zealand in Barefoot Waterskiing at four World Championships. As an athlete, he honed the critical skill of 'stilling the mind', enabling peak performance. This skill, amongst many others, he now passes onto his clients as 'the way' to overcome most modern-day leader's challenges.

Timothy has featured in numerous newspapers and magazines articles, on leadership podcasts, and has extensive blog and newsletter publications. He serves on the board of Lend a Hand Bahamas (LAHB), a non-profit organisation focused on community & youth development. Since opening the community centre in 2018, LAHB has positively influenced the lives of thousands of children and their families. Timothy currently resides in the Bahamas with his family.

The Evolutionary Leader – 5 Steps to Dramatically Develop People and Performance

In his role of developing leaders worldwide, Timothy discusses the biggest challenges leaders face and provides solutions to overcome them.

Are you a successful business owner or leader struggling to maintain a balanced life, experiencing stress, and feeling unproductive? Is your work-life balance teetering, affecting your personal relationships? Perhaps you find yourself entangled in the day-to-day operations of your business, rather than it operating efficiently under your guidance. What you truly desire is more time and financial freedom, the ability to achieve more with less effort, and an improved quality of life. This yearning might stem from a nagging sense that something is missing, a gap within you that wants to be filled.

I often begin my leadership trainings with a simple yet revealing question: "How many of you would like your life back?" Almost invariably, 80% of the participants raise their hands. This pattern is evident among business leaders worldwide: many have not learned to effectively lead themselves, let alone their teams. Most people start a business to create more wealth or gain more time with family, but in reality, they're searching for more freedom. The question is, how's that quest working out for you?

As a young man, I studied architectural drafting and building sciences and worked for an architectural firm in New Zealand, contributing significantly to their revenue while earning a modest salary. I was not fulfilled and after going through a mid-life crisis in my early 20's where I lost everything, I decided to pack up and travel the world to find myself.

My journey eventually led me to Sydney, Australia, where I had the opportunity to assist renowned authors and trainers like Tony Robbins and Dr Stephen Covey amongst many others. It was during this time that I felt inspired to serve humanity in a similar way. You become who you associate with, so after training with world leaders in the field of cognitive behavioural sciences and coaching, I established my own business.

Several years later, I noticed a recurring pattern: a lack of time and financial freedom, and unfulfilled core values. This realization pushed me to make a change. It's a story that many entrepreneurs and family business owners can relate to – their business ends up owning them rather than them owning their business. So, ask yourself: does your business own you, or do you have the time and financial freedom you desire, with a business that works for you?

In these tumultuous times, the world faces challenges such as ongoing conflicts in Ukraine and Palestine, increasing political polarization, rising inflation and interest rates, social unrest, and predictions of worsening global instability that make the future uncertain. As business leaders, we already carry the weight of managing our business, without the added burden of potential crises.

Business leaders and owners must find ways to manage current stressors, build resilience against future challenges, and ensure their businesses are prepared for potential setbacks. This chapter's purpose is to guide you through the rough seas and help you reach safe harbor. By mastering the skills and mindset shared here, you can consistently navigate these challenges and outperform your competition.

One thing is certain: when you're on your deathbed, you won't wish you had worked more. You'll wish you had more time and resources to spend with your loved ones. This chapter aims to empower and support you in overcoming some of the most significant problems you face as a leader and in your business. IIt's about reclaiming control, not only of your business but also of your life.

With over two decades of research and extensive work with leaders worldwide, I've uncovered a universal key. One thing that can help you achieve your goals and more right now. That key is "presence," the ability to fully inhabit the here and now.

At this point, I must share a significant turning point in my journey which occurred during my days as a competitive barefoot water-skier. I vividly recall a crucial tournament in Florida, a week before the World Championships. The day was perfect, the sun sparkled on the glassy water, and as the boat moved away from the dock, I gave my instructions to the driver and dived into the water. The rope went tight, I shouted, "Hit it!" and the boat powered away. I stood up and a few seconds later I had completed my trick run seamlessly and skied to the end of the lake.

As I threw the handle away and sunk into the water, my mind said to me, that was so good, but I bet you will fall off next pass. How many of you reading this right now have had an automatic negative thought like that? I lay there struggling with this thought that infected my mind like a virus. All I could think, see, and feel was me falling off.

The boat inevitably returned for my next run, I couldn't escape the negative thought and as predicted, I fell on a basic trick. This experience proved life-altering, unveiling the power of our thoughts in shaping our results. What we focus on determines our outcomes. A still mind was the secret to peak performance. I had experienced it during my first pass when my mind was clear and present. The second pass, dominated by a negative thought, produced a different result.

I went to colleagues of mine in my sport and asked them, "Hey, what are you thinking about when you're skiing? When you break that personal best, or exceed your potential in a big tournament? What are you thinking about?" And all of them said, "I'm not thinking about anything!" They had the same experience as me. When asking other people, it didn't matter if they were a water-skier or a pianist, or a runner, or an artist, all of them had no mind. A no-mind experience.

So, what is no mind? What is this state of being? Its presence and presence is the key to your success. The ability to be here right now, in this moment, is the number one thing that—when you get it—will support you to have the best life possible.

This revelation served to create a paradigm shift in my life. I became committed to understanding how to be fully present and still my mind to unlock my full potential. It was a pivotal moment for me, prompting me to find a new way of operating in the world.

Today's world calls for leadership as volatility continues to grow. Leaders are needed now more than ever. The skills that are required go beyond traditional business acumen; they encompass personal mastery, resilience, and a strong mental immune system to tackle future uncertainties.

If you've reached a point in your life where enough is enough and you're ready to make a change to regain control, you're in the right place. We are calling upon individuals who are ready to step across the line, join a community of like-minded individuals, and embark on a journey of growth and evolution as leaders. We seek those who are committed to becoming the best versions of themselves and creating the results they truly desire.

The world needs a different type of leader today, and I'll even go as far to say, a new type of human being. One that is more evolved, who leads from a place of self-mastery, devoid of an ego-driven mind. This leader understands the importance of presence, the ability to be fully in the moment. Most leaders and most human beings are run by their mind and their emotions. It is their mind and emotions that determine their communication and behaviour. And the mind is running on automatic like it was for me when I was in that competition in Florida.

Are you running your mind? Or is your mind running you? And what is the way to get back in charge, back in the driver's seat?

If it is running you, the good news is, that I'm here to tell you there is a way to solve the challenges and problems you're facing right now. And what if there was one way, one way which takes care of it all? In the following pages, I will help you to learn that way, and how to do it. So that you can start to put it into practice and get the results you desire. What results? Much greater levels of fulfilment and freedom.

At the beginning of this chapter, there was a question I mentioned I asked first thing in my leadership trainings. "How many people here want their life back?" And I'm guessing many of you when reading this put your hands up. It's time to embark on a journey to unlock your full potential, achieve better health, make better decisions, improve your relationships, and experience more fulfillment. The key to all of this is presence, the ability to be fully here and now.

We are human beings, not human doings. However, many of us have lost touch with our true selves and become engrossed in constant busyness, often driven by technology. We must learn to be human beings again. In the middle of a pandemic, I accidentally lost my smartphone in the sea. Unable to replace it for several weeks, I discovered I could operate my business and live life without it, emphasizing that being is more valuable than doing.

"Yesterday is history. Tomorrow is a mystery. Today is a gift.
That's why its called the present." – **Alice Morse Earle**

Today, I offer you the gift of presence. Drawing from over 25 years of experience working with diverse individuals and organizations, I've identified patterns of thinking, feeling, communication, and behaviour that lead to specific undesired results. The one solution that addresses these patterns is the gift of presence.

The big question is: how do you learn to silence your mind, do less, and achieve more? How do you become fully present, experiencing the gap between thoughts, the silence that allows for peak performance?

Just Be It

The first step is to still your mind, which requires dedicating time to simply be. Paradoxically, the busier you are, the more essential it is to schedule "being time." When you're busy, you must find time to be in the midst of constant doing. Practice "just being" in the morning and evening. Meditate, if you will. This stillness helps you set the tone for a successful day and helps you wind down in the evening. Don't just do it, as the saying goes – just be it. Being precedes doing; be present, and you will naturally do what is necessary and attain what you desire.

The first thing you want to do is make sure you have a quiet space at home where you can sit comfortably and not be disturbed. Make this place the one place you will always sit at in the mornings and evenings. Sit upright, with a straight back, hands facing up on your lap. Then take three deep breaths in through your nose and out through your nose. You'll notice that those breaths with practice will come from your belly. Breathe into your belly deeply several times until you notice your mind and body start to relax and let go. This activates the parasympathetic nervous system that supports you in releasing stress. Then continue to breathe normally, in through your nose and out through your nose, and focus on your breath.

There are three things that can happen while you are sitting there focusing on your breath:

1. **The first thing is you fall asleep.** That's okay, it's your neurology catching up on sleep and it's just feedback that you need to get to bed earlier. The hours between 10pm and 2am are very important as this is when your physical body heals.
2. **You can have a lot of turbulence in your mind, a lot of thoughts that kick in and you get caught up in those thoughts**. If you get distracted with your thoughts, catch yourself and come back to focusing on the breath moving in and out through your nose. The activity in your mind is stress being released and the longer you sit the more stress you let go of. In fact, universities around the world have found that meditation is the number one thing you can do to release stress from your mind and body.
3. **Lastly, you can have a no-mind experience and the mind becomes quiet and still.** Here you can directly experience more peace, harmony, and fulfillment inside.

The recommendation is to do this in the morning and the evening around sunrise and sunset. It is a special time of the day when it is naturally still and peaceful outside. I recommend sitting for a period of five minutes to start with and do this every day for a week. Then increase it every week by five minutes until you reach twenty minutes. Twenty minutes is the minimum time found for you to gain the benefits of meditation.

Benefits of Scheduled Being Time

Decades of scientific studies done on meditation have proven that:

1. **It directly releases stress from the body and mind.**
2. **That long term meditators are much more able to cope with stress.**

3. **People who meditate can go into a relaxing state twice as deep as deep sleep.** And this can happen in ten minutes, compared to four to six hours when we are sleeping.
4. **That biological age is reversed through meditation.** Robert Wallace at UCLA California found that people who had meditated for five years or more have a biological age on average 12 years younger than their actual age.
5. **Our health improves.** A health study done on a group of 2000 people who meditate showed that they were hospitalized for heart disease 87% less often than non-meditators and were hospitalized 50% less often for cancer. The people were also much healthier than the average population in 17 major areas of serious disease, both mental and physical.
6. **Meditation improves our ability to focus, our creativity, our learning ability, and even our memory.**
7. **Meditation creates more harmony and gives us more energy and a deep sense of fulfillment in our lives.**
8. **Meditation supports us in coming into the now and staying in the present in the midst of dynamic activity, where peak performance comes from.**

The practice of taking the time to just be every day is conditioning your nervous system. You're telling your nervous system, "This is how I want to be in the world." By practicing it in the morning, you set up yourself for success for the day. And in the evening, you release the day and wind down for the evening.

It's a great practice to keep a journal and track your progress. In the journal, I would write out the time you began sitting. How long you sat for. What your experience was while sitting. And at the end of the day, also note down how your day was and how your practice helped you. For example, were you more present? Were you able to accept situations and circumstances more easily? Did you have more energy and focus?

Taking your Ability to Just Be to the Next Level

The key is to take your ability to be present into every moment. Sure, taking the time to just be in the morning, and the evening is going to have great benefits for you. The practice to really master is the ability to be present in every moment.

When there's a lot of inner turbulence and your thoughts are running the game and in charge, the gap between the thoughts is very small. It's an endless stream of thought. And when you're present, in contrast, there are no thoughts, the mind is still and the gap between the thoughts is big. The silence between your thoughts is what you want to expand and dive into.

Many years ago, I was in Sweden, and a good friend of mine, William Trubridge—a multiple world record holder in freediving—came through Malmo as he was holding a training in Sweden. We sat down over a cup of tea, and I was super curious to find out what his experience was when he was diving. At that time, William had broken the world record, in the purest form of freediving, constant weight; no fins, just him and his breath, diving down to over 82 meters deep or 269 feet.

I asked him, "Hey, William, what are you thinking about when you're diving", and he said, "Sometimes when I'm breathing up on the surface, I have a thought that comes into my mind, this is going to be my last breath. And sometimes I have a thought when I'm diving, hey, turn back, you're going to die."

I asked him, "So what do you do with those thoughts?"

He said, "Well, after many years of diving, I realized that those thoughts don't serve me. So, I don't pay attention to them anymore."

And I asked him, "So what are you paying attention to when you're diving?"

He said, "I'm paying attention to the silence between my thoughts, the gap, and the deeper that I dive into that gap between my thoughts, the more present I can be, the deeper I can actually dive into the ocean."

That blew my mind. Today, William has evolved himself and his ability to dive much deeper. He has pushed out the world record to 102m, or 334.6 feet.

Here are three practical tools that have worked well for me and for the people that I've worked with, to help them take presence into their everyday life.

1. **Listening** - The practice of listening is very powerful. It's the reason God gave us two ears and one mouth, because we need to listen twice as much as we talk during the day. The greatest need for a human being is to feel heard, met and understood. This happens when you proactively listen to people. And by proactive, I mean that you're not thinking about a response to what the person is saying. You are present in their presence and really taking in their words and their communication. One trick is to listen with your eyes. Be hyper-externally focused on them. It's a trick elite athletes use to tap into the now.

2. **Acceptance** – Sometimes we can get triggered by situations, circumstances, or people. The practice is to accept everything as it is. Jiddu Krishnamurti once said, *"The highest form of human intelligence is to observe everything without judgment."* Try that for five minutes. Try to accept everything as it is, not as you wish it to be. When triggered, there is a resistance to what is. This creates an emotional response, e-motion, energy in motion. The trick is to breathe through it. Every emotion has a beginning, middle and end and breathing helps the energy to flow and not get stuck. We can allow these emotions and energy to take us over or we can master the energy and allow it to flow.
3. **Breath Worship** – Just like when you focus on your breathing during meditation. The opportunity is to take the time to focus on your breath during the day. Be present with your breath moving in and out through your nose as much as you can during the day. Now, that's a challenge. You're going to get distracted by your thoughts. The key is to catch yourself and come back to your breath. Condition yourself every day, in every way, in every moment, to be still, to be present.

"Lose your mind and come to your senses." – **Fritz Perls**

Breath worship is an amazing practice that will support you in being present throughout the whole day. You can practice it with colleagues, family, and friends, and by that, I mean hold each other accountable. Keep track of how well you have been able to achieve it during the day.

Your Next Step Towards Mastery

You now possess the tools to infuse presence into your everyday existence. Presence is the number one skill that can solve most of the challenges you face. By mastering it, you'll experience better health, happiness, fulfillment, and the ability to perform at your best, just like world-class athletes, musicians, and artists.

Are you ready to become an Evolutionary Leader? These leaders challenge the status quo for themselves and for others, they lead by example, and are driven by a higher purpose. Join our community of Evolutionary Leaders and embark on a journey to self-mastery, where we support one another in evolving and reaching our full potential.

As you conclude this chapter, my hope is that you are inspired to tackle the one thing that may be hindering your growth – your own mind. The information and tools provided here are designed to help you elevate your life and work towards the results that you desire.

The choice is yours: do you want to settle for less, or do you want to pursue what you truly desire? Don't settle for less than your aspirations. As a dear friend once told me: "If you settle for less than what you want, you'll always get less than what you settle for."

So, what is it that you truly desire? What do you really want? If mastering one thing could make all the difference in your life, your business, your closest relationships, and your well-being, wouldn't you go for it? I believe in your ability to master this secret of success. You got this!

To book Timothy for your stage or podcast, reach out to his assistant at support@carrollconsultancy.com to find a time to discuss the opportunity.

Join Timothy and his community of Evolutionary Leaders today by scanning the QR code below or go to *www.theevolutionaryleaders.com* where you will find your gift and the next steps on how you can start your journey towards self-mastery today.

www.ingramcontent.com/pod-product-compliance
Lightning Source LLC
LaVergne TN
LVHW010933100826
845153LV00001B/20

* 9 7 8 0 6 4 8 6 2 3 1 8 2 *